Skira**M**ini**ART**books

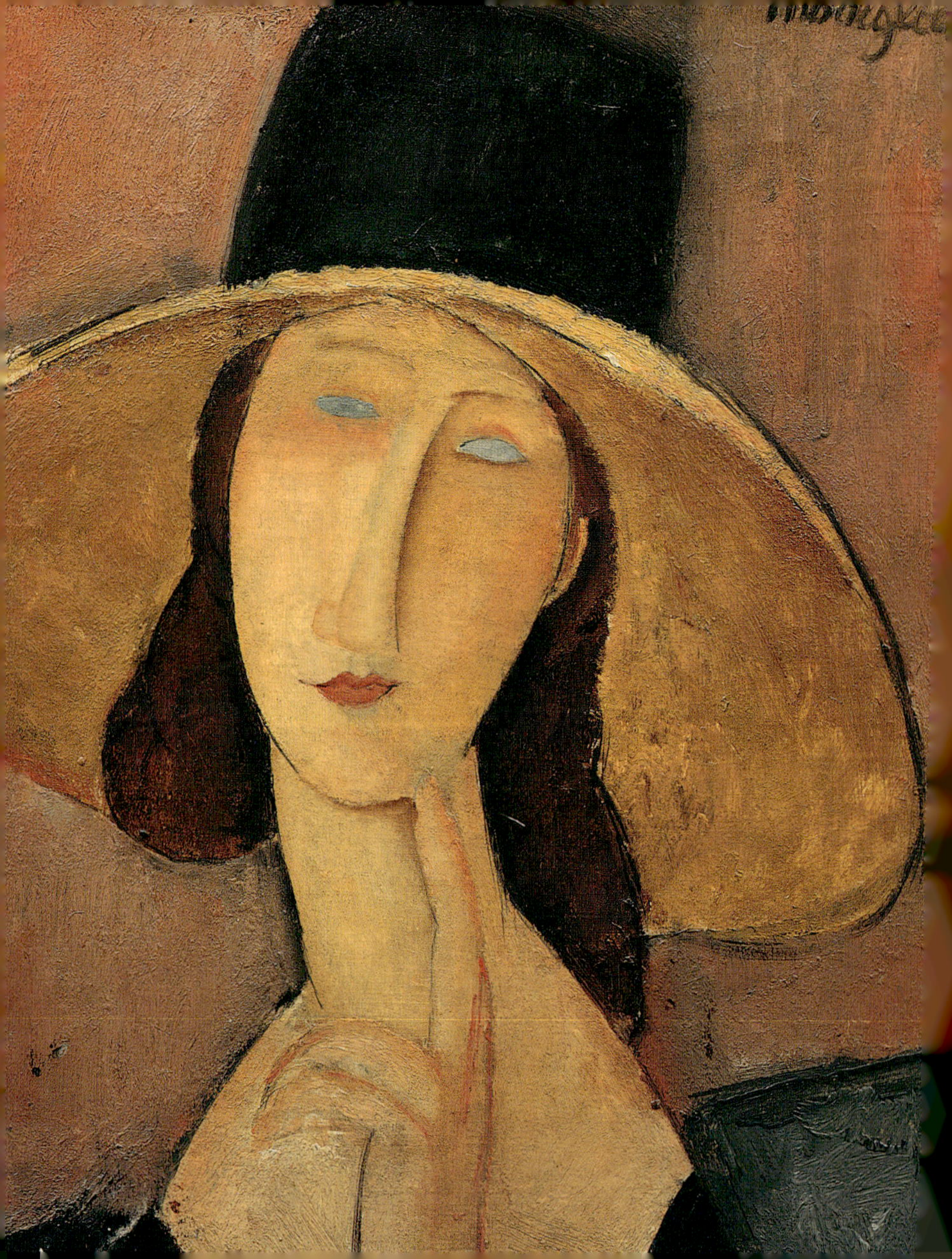

Francesca Marini

MODIGLIANI

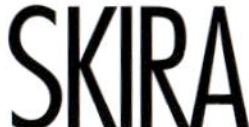

Front cover
Sleeping Nude with Arms Open
(Red Nude) (detail), 1917
Oil on canvas, 60 x 92 cm
Mattioli Collection, Milan

Editor
Eileen Romano

Design
Marcello Francone

Editorial Coordination
Giovanna Rocchi

Editing
Maria Conconi

Layout
Anna Cattaneo

Iconographical Research
Alice Spadacini

Translation
Christopher "Shanti" Evans
for Language Consulting
Congressi, Milan

First published in Italy in 2009
by Skira Editore S.p.A.
Palazzo Casati Stampa
via Torino 61
20123 Milano
Italy

www.skira.net

Printed and bound in Italy.
First edition

ISBN 978-88-572-0045-0

Distributed in the US and Canada
through Rizzoli International
Publications by Random House,
300 Park Avenue South,
New York, NY 10010.
Distributed elsewhere in the world
by Thames and Hudson Ltd.,
181a High Holborn, London
WC1V 7QX, United Kingdom.

Facing title page
Jeanne Hébuterne
in a Large Hat (detail), 1918
Oil on canvas, 55 x 38 cm
Private collection, Japan

On page 84
Jeanne Hébuterne
with Hat and Necklace
(detail), 1917
Private collection

© Foto Archivio Scala, Firenze,
2009

Contents

Modigliani

On the 12 July, 1884, Eugénie Garsin went into labour. She was expecting her fourth child. The family which was bringing Amedeo Modigliani into the world was in dire financial straits, following the failure of the company that handled trade in wood and coal and the exploitation of several mines in Sardinia and that had almost always kept Flaminio Modigliani, Amedeo's father and Eugénie's husband, far away from home.

Amedeo Modigliani was the youngest of the children and showed no particular artistic inclinations, but in the summer of 1895, after recording the appearance of the first of the frequent illnesses that were going to blight the life of the future painter, his mother prophetically hit the mark when she wrote: "We shall have to wait and see what is inside this chrysalis. Perhaps an artist?" The answer was to come very soon. After not very brilliant results in his high-school exams, Eugénie Garsin agreed to enrol her son Amedeo in the drawing course "which he had been longing to do for some time" and which was to commence in August 1897.

Legend has it that two years later, in the grip of fever, the young Modigliani had wrung permission from his mother to give up his studies for good in order to devote himself exclusively to painting, consumed by the creative fire of art at the age of just fourteen. Subsequently he began to frequent the studio of Guglielmo Micheli in Livorno. Amedeo Modigliani is said to have been a respectful pupil, willing to adopt the approach of the Macchiaiolo painter and to explore the Tuscan countryside and the working-class districts of Livorno with brushes and easel in line with the best tradition of the movement, and in the company of other young artists. Some of these, such as Oscar Ghiglia or Renato Natali, diverging like Amedeo from the post-Macchiaiolo vein from which they had all started out, were later to enjoy a considerable reputation, although nothing to match what awaited Modigliani after his move to Paris. After a while, however, Micheli's studio was no longer sufficient for Amedeo: Florence was not far from Livorno, but offered a far more stimulating environment.

In Florence, in addition, there was his friend from Livorno Oscar Ghiglia, and the elderly Giovanni Fattori was running the "Scuola Libera di Nudo" in a dingy and poorly heated attic. Modigliani enrolled at the school on 7 May 1902. During his short stay in Florence, Modigliani got a flavour of the cosmopolitan climate that he was to find in Paris, sharing a studio with Ghiglia and meeting other young artists, including Ortiz de Zárate, with whom he formed a friendship that was destined to grow stronger in the years in Paris. And it is conceivable that it was in this period that Modigliani first came into contact with his favourite material, stone, from which he was to carve his famous heads and caryatids many years later.

In March 1903 Modigliani moved to Venice, where the city's first international exhibition of art had been held only eight years earlier.

A few months after his arrival in Venice it seems that Amedeo still had "the fine and delicate appearance of a handsome adolescent of good family, well dressed and sensible". He said he was in the city "to study the graceful manner of Giovanni Bellini, Carpaccio, and some of the Sienese" of the 14th century, and combined his academic activity with work in the studio he had rented opposite San Sebastiano.

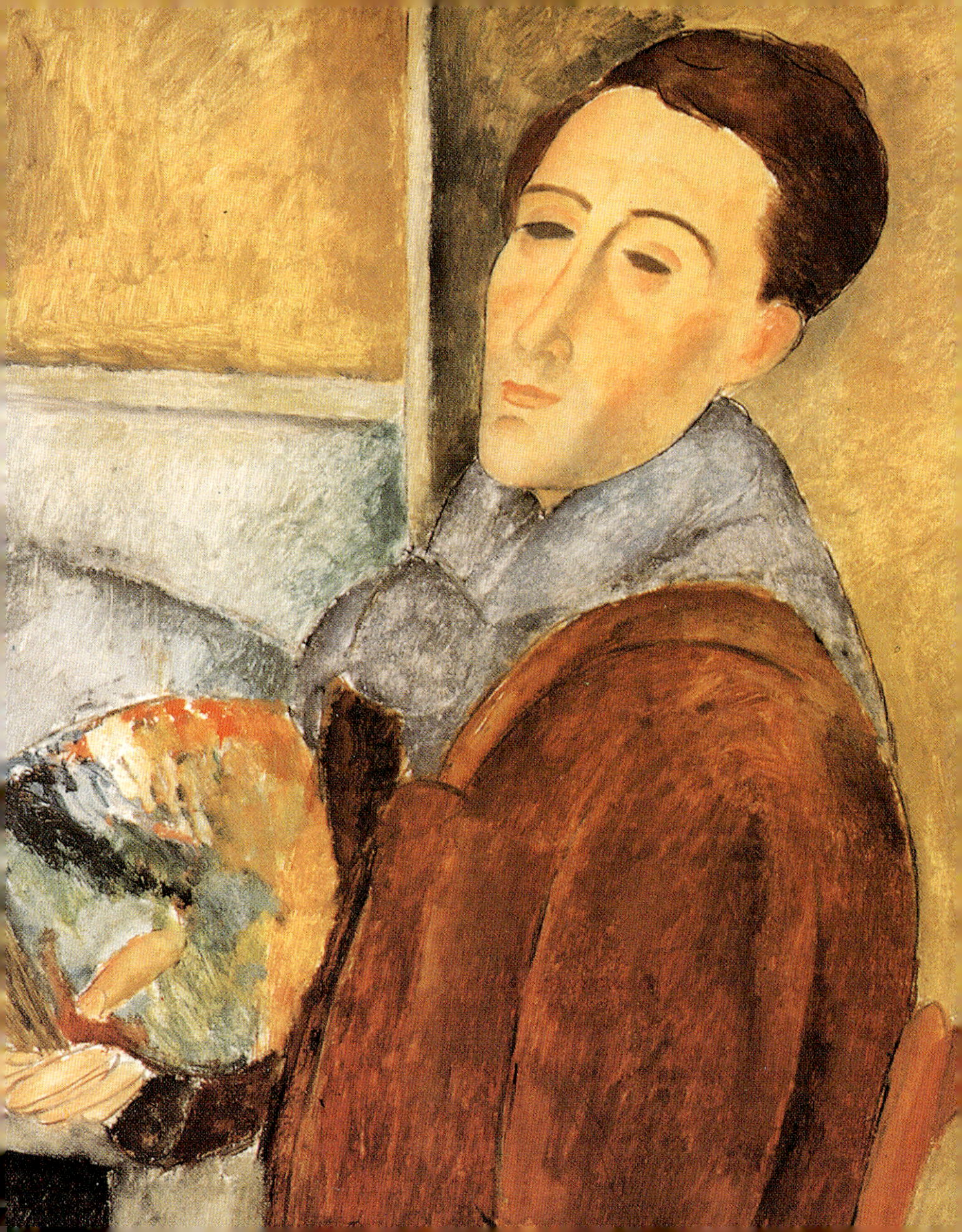

"Modigliani had a taste for danger.
He thought that one should not be
afraid to risk one's life in order
to expand it. Utterly despising
mediocrity, he had pretension
to royal privilege."

Paul Alexandre

At the end of 1905 Eugénie Garsin went to Venice to see her son and, despite the death of his uncle Amédée Garsin, who had funded Modigliani's studies up till then, brought with her a bundle of books and the money he needed to fulfil his desire to move to Paris.

Sure that he was going to get on there easily thanks to his perfect command of the language, Amedeo left Venice for Paris in the cold winter months of 1906.

Montmartre seemed the right place to live, not only because the quarter had become celebrated as the haunt of all the young artists drawn to the city by the fame of the Impressionists, but also because a studio in Montmartre was inexpensive. In addition, the one Modigliani rented in Rue Caulaincourt was right next to some buildings under construction, where plenty of stone was lying around, allowing him to obtain the raw material for his sculptures with great ease and at low cost.

Enrolling at the Académie Colarossi in Rue de la Grande Chaumière, where he would go on learning and practising, Modigliani, dressed in a loose-fitting velvet jacket in the style of the Maremma, with a red scarf around his neck and a broad-brimmed hat on his head, immediately introduced himself into the life of Montmartre, that of "La Butte", the highest part of the quarter. Here, around Place du Tertre and the church of the Sacré Coeur, nearing completion, there were construction sites, vegetable gardens and ramshackle huts and sheds where street urchins hung around, the down-and-outs of the city lived and young artists could find a place to stay for very little.

The real art school in Paris was to be found in the city's cafés, bistros, cabarets and taverns, where the most heated discussions of art, poetry and music were conducted and the new spirits of the 20th century used to meet. Within a short time Modigliani had got to know Pablo Picasso, André Derain, the poet Guillaume Apollinaire, Diego Rivera, Max Jacob and Jacques Lipchitz. Artists and poets from all over Europe, still looking for their own direction in art.

With the completion of the new buildings Modigliani was obliged to give up his studio in Rue Caulaincourt and, after wandering from the hôtel du Poirier to one in Place du Tertre, lived for a while at the Bateau-Lavoir until he managed to rent the workshop of a carpenter, a flimsy construction of roof tiles and wood at number 7, Place Clément.

Modigliani had not arrived in Paris with a total lack of cultural grounding, as the Venetian artistic milieu had left him with a good understanding of the most recent developments in Symbolism and Art Nouveau, but it had certainly not prepared him for the sensational innovations of the Fauves, Matisse, Derain and Vlaminck, who had just shown their works at the Salon des Indépendants and the Salon d'Automne, or for the ones that would lead to the development of Cubism and Expressionism.

Modigliani in those years was still stubbornly trying to find his own way. Dissatisfied, he destroyed his works and declared he wanted to devote himself to sculpture. The Tuscan painter Anselmo Bucci said that one winter evening in 1906, walking past the Art Gallery, a little shop almost on the corner of Rue des Saints-Pères and Boulevard Saint-Germain run by the English poetess Laura Wylda, he saw in the window "three wan and haunted women's faces, almost monochrome, painted in pale green earth on small canvases". As far as we know this was the first time that any of Modigliani's works had been exposed to the eyes of the public in Paris.

The first turning-point in Modigliani's artistic career came after his meeting with Paul and Jean Alexandre. In 1907 Paul Alexandre, who was to become a famous surgeon, was still a specialist in internal diseases at the Lariboisière hospital and his brother Jean was finishing his studies to become a pharmacist. Both were art lovers and would rent a run-down house at number 7, Rue du Delta, in order to provide artists with a cheap, and sometimes free, place to live and work. Two people with more expertise, the sculptor Drouart and the painter Doucet, were given the task of choosing which artists should be given access to this space. It was they who arranged the first meeting between Amedeo Modigliani and Paul Alexandre, and the doctor immediately suggested he move to the house on Rue du Delta. Modigliani did not change his residence, but took his books and pictures there and sold a portrait entitled *The Jewess* to Paul. Paul Alexandre was still not earning much as a doctor, but tried to buy pictures from Modigliani regularly so that he could survive, paying him each time whatever he could afford, from twenty centimes to twenty francs, although the sum he paid for *The Jewess* was exceptionally high. In this way the young doctor built up a collection of around twenty-five pictures and many drawings by Modigliani over the years.

It seems that Alexandre was captivated by Modigliani, with whom he had lively discussions about Toulouse-Lautrec, Boldini and the exhibitions by Cézanne and Matisse that they had visited together. It was Paul Alexandre who introduced Modigliani to the primitive arts of Africa, America, Mesopotamia and Oceania on show in the Guimet, Louvre and Trocadéro museums, opening up new horizons for him. And it was Alexandre again who, as his doctor and friend, and de-

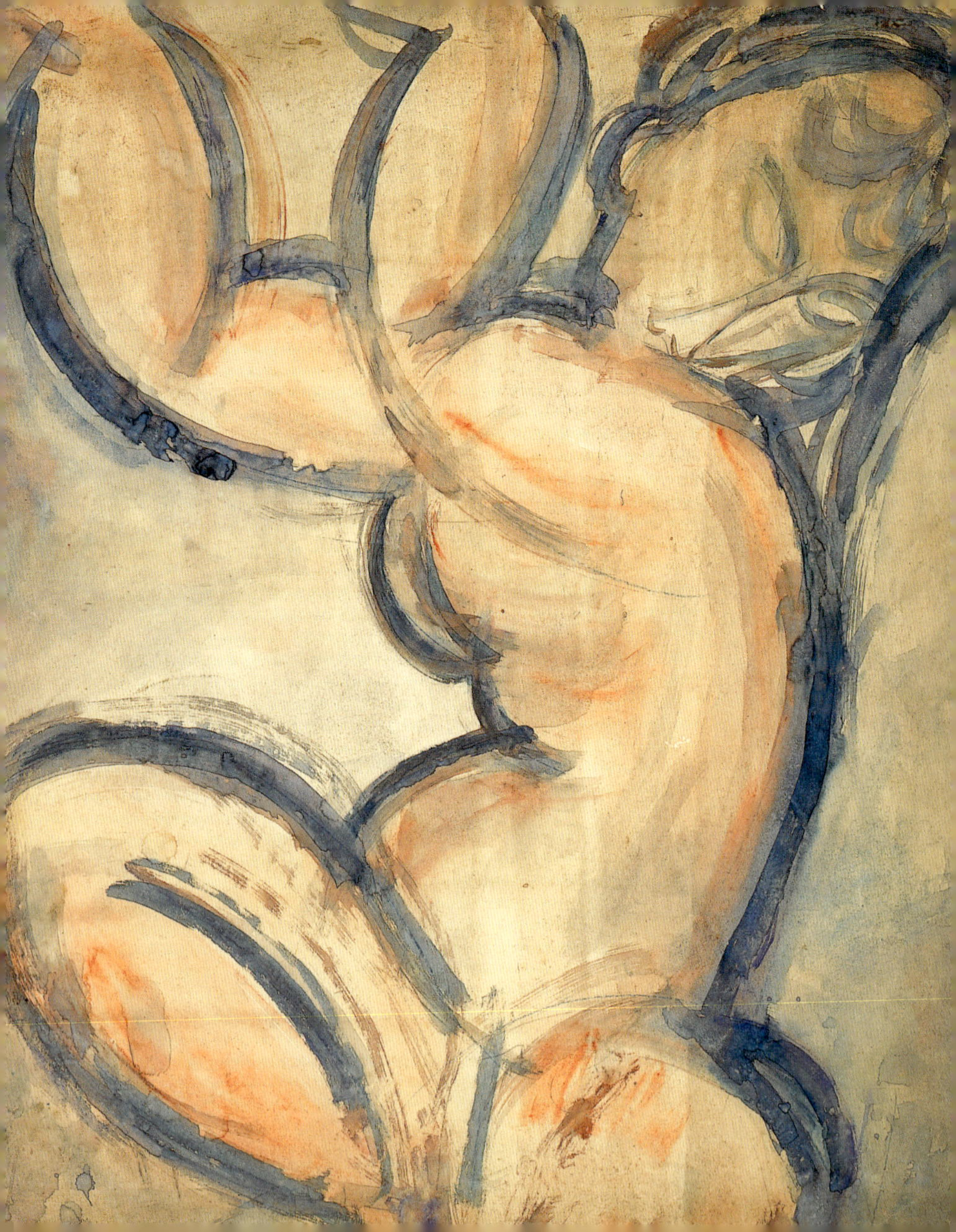

spite praising the capacities of hashish as a means of heightening sensations, disapproved of Modigliani's excesses in the use of alcohol and drugs. These excesses, which in reality were typical of the experimentation carried out by many young artists in those years, did not tarnish Paul Alexandre's view of Modigliani as "a very well-educated young man, believe me, despite everything that has been written". But a young man who needed guidance and encouragement. And so at the end of 1907 the doctor, conscious of the important role played by official institutions in bringing an artist to the public's attention, persuaded Modigliani to put his name down for the Salon des Indépendants, an exhibition in which anyone could take part without having to go through screening by a jury. The exhibition was held in March 1908 and Amedeo Modigliani showed five works, including *The Jewess.*

According to Charles-Albert Cingria, Modigliani "certainly drank and sometimes became animated, but neither more nor less than others at that time (…). I have rarely seen him exceed the normal dose permitted to any civilized being, that is to say a litre with a meal" (1934). Besides, when money is short, meals are scanty, and on an empty stomach wine goes to the head. On top of all this, the effect of Modigliani's premature death was to give rise to tales and stories on the part of any witness to the life of the time. The numerous anecdotes and memoirs of far too many people have embroidered Modigliani's life, contributing to the myth of the genius struck down at the height of his creativity and displacing accurate reconstructions by the image of the artist as the last *poète maudit,* perpetually seeking self-destruction. Yet we know that legends always have a kernel of truth and there can be no doubt that Modigliani used drugs, chiefly hashish, and drank without worrying about the consequences.

The dozens of drawings that Modigliani made in that period consist both of carefully thought-out studies and rapid sketches of friends, done during discussions in cafés and taverns. The progressive purification of the forms towards which Modigliani was moving, using a single, slender and unbroken line in his drawings, was aimed at capturing the essence of volumes, movements and expressions that the artist felt an urgent need to attain through sculpture as well. He had never given up the idea of working in sculpture. The painter Henri Doucet tells us that, at the time he lived in Place Clément, Modigliani had decided to get hold of wood for his sculptures to avoid the dust and labour that working with stone entailed. So Doucet was persuaded by Modigliani to help him find the material, and ended up having to climb over the fence of the Barbés-Rochechouart Métro station, still under construction, to steal the sleepers from a track which were then used to create works that it has not proved possible to trace. The primitive art to which Paul Alexandre had introduced him had opened up a whole new world.

In reality in those days far more was included in the category of primitive art than can really be considered such, and in practice everything that preceded the Greek civilization was lumped together under the concept of primitivism, including the art of ancient Egypt and Africa, which both played an essential role in the process of Modigliani's maturation. Drawing and painting were solutions subordinated to a single problem that could only be solved with sculpture, a medium that had become inescapable for the artist. However, the fact remained that the cost of the material, the objective difficulties of the technique which required physical effort and suitable premises, his delicate health and the pressure from dealers and patrons who were more willing to buy pictures and drawings than sculptures slowed down the work, which often entailed dozens and dozens of preparatory drawings before he laid his hands directly on the piece of stone.

Nonetheless Modigliani would try his hand at the execution of sculptures on various occasions and in different locations, up until 1916: works of which probably only part have survived and which, apart from a few exceptions, can still not be arranged today in clear chronological order. After Modigliani had to leave the studio in Place Clément, a period of frequent moves began during which he found it hard to take anything cumbersome with him. To the lack of a permanent home were added other problems caused by the life he led and, after he had destroyed the works of some other artists one evening, "drunk on wine and rage", he was expelled from Rue du Delta.

Fortunately he found refuge at La Ruche, "The Beehive". La Ruche was located in the Passage Dantzig in Paris's 15th arrondissement and had been created by the sculptor Alfred Boucher in 1902. Ardengo Soffici, who had lived there from 1903 to 1905, recalls that while at the outset the tenants of La Ruche were largely "mediocre artists", "painters of potboilers, forgers of religious images, wood-engravers for catalogues and illustrated dictionaries", later Chagall, Soutine, Léger, Archipenko and Modigliani arrived, attracted by the modest rents and by the wholly international character of the place.

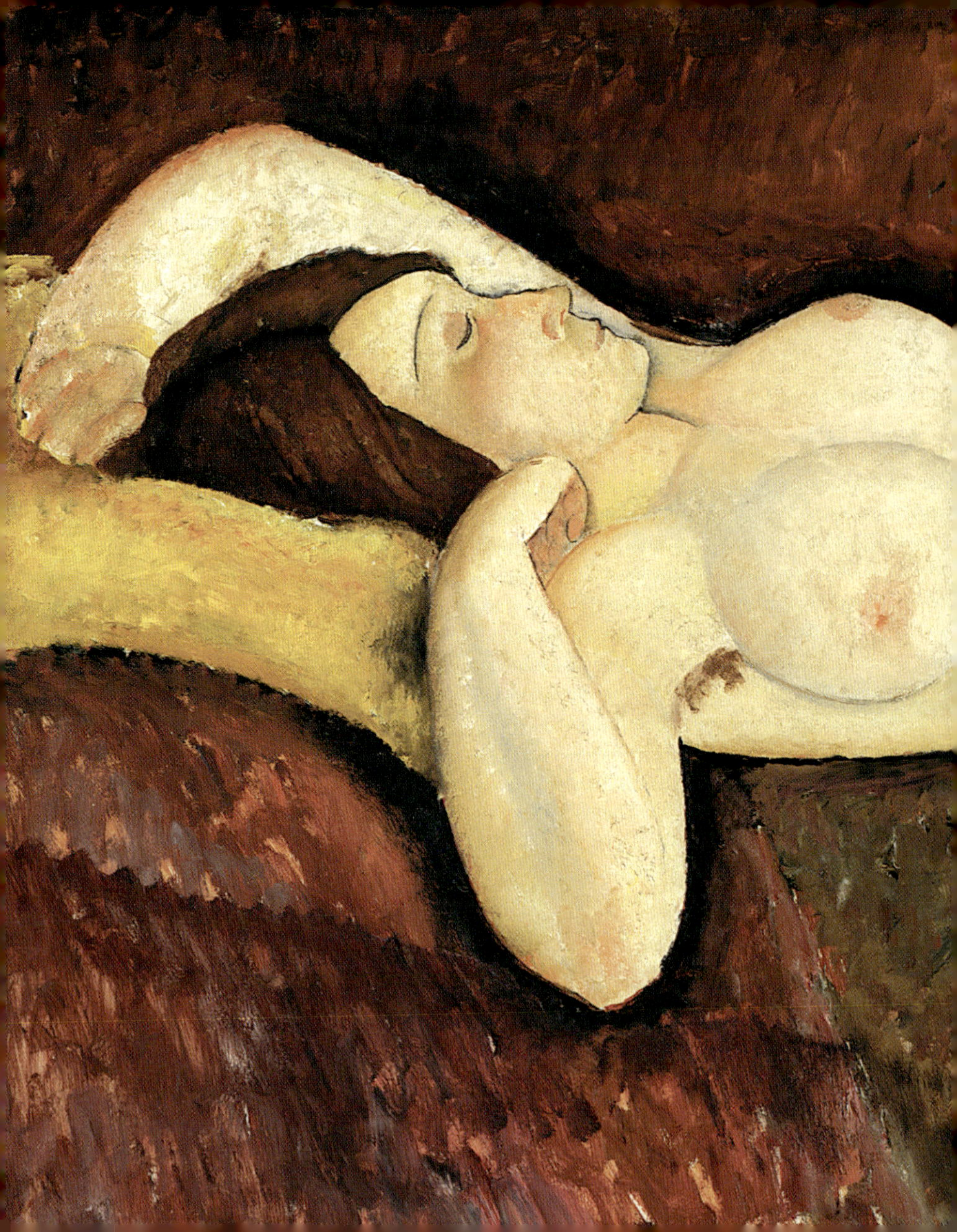

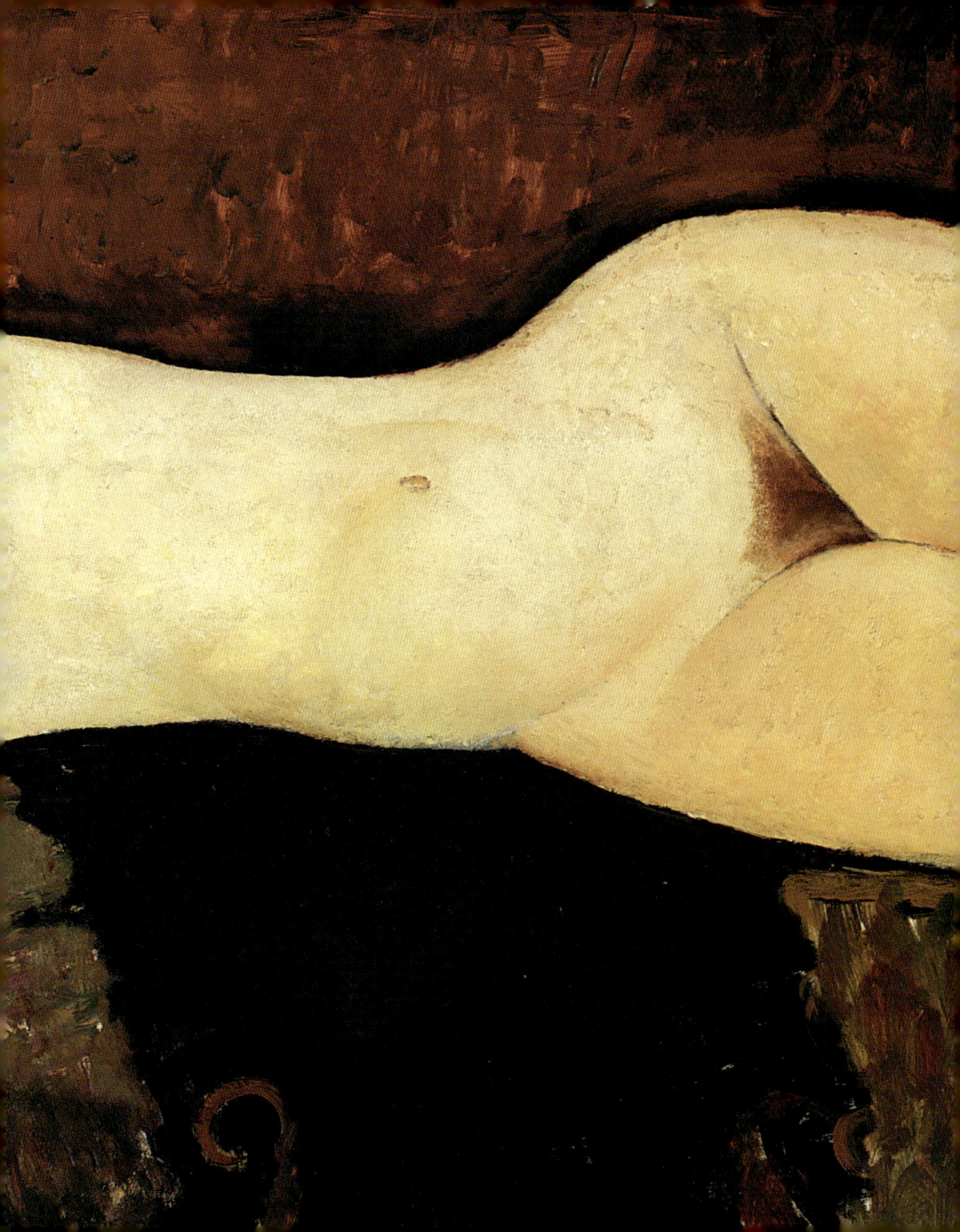

By the end of 1909 Modigliani had moved again. He was now living on the first floor of a shack with a tin roof at number 14, Cité Falguière, known as the "Ville Rose" for the colour of the walls of the main building. This is probably where he painted *The Cellist*, using as a model a friend who was able to take advantage of the heat of the woodstove to practise on his instrument during the sittings for the portrait (Jeanne Modigliani, 1958).

In 1911 his association with Constantin Brancusi and friendship with Amadeo de Souza-Cardoso led to Modigliani holding his first exhibition of sculptures. We do not know exactly when Cardoso and Modigliani met. It may have been through their common friend Max Jacob, who knew everyone, or perhaps they just ran into one another in Montparnasse. A few photographs of the exhibition have come down to us, allowing us to see which works Modigliani chose to show to the public. The pictures are of elongated heads, faces furrowed by the vertical geometry of the nose and the swollen ovals of the eyes, essential and absolute forms that were the fruit of his long discussions with Constantin Brancusi.

The Romanian sculptor was eight years older than Modigliani and already fairly well-known in Paris. He tried to remain true to his own traditions, going around dressed in a smock and with clogs on his feet. He preferred not to hang around the Rive Gauche, but kept company instead with Jean Cocteau, Apollinaire or Raymond Radiguet, passing his evenings on the other bank of the Seine, perhaps at the performances of the Ballets Russes staged by the brilliant impresario Diaghilev or playing the violin with "Le Douanier" Rousseau. It was Brancusi who provided Modigliani with a new key to sculpture, advising him from the technical point of view as well as discussing

Rodin with him. He also went with him to look at what examples the Paris of those years had to offer of primitive art, African art and ancient Egyptian sculpture, with the aim of studying in depth these artefacts, which had such a decisive influence on many of the artists of the day. Brancusi's portrait appears on the back of a study made in 1909 for *The Cellist*. The sculptor is represented with a thick beard, a prominent, sharp and curved nose and dark and deep-set eyes in shadow under the broad and imposing forehead: a sort of painted sculpture. In those years sculpture appears to have completely dominated Modigliani's output, and he also seems to have steered his friend Jacques Lipchitz in the direction of ancient Egyptian plastic art.

When Anna Akhmatova met Modigliani she was only twenty, and despite the fact that they only saw each other a few times, Modigliani wrote to her right through the winter before meeting her again in Paris the following year. According to Anna Akhmatova "Parisian painting had swallowed up French poetry" at the beginning of the 20th century, and on a bench in the Jardin du Luxembourg she and Amedeo Modigliani used to recite Verlaine together, "happy to remember the same poems".

In 1911 Anna Akhmatova had found him "completely darkened, emaciated". Modigliani was so poor that "it was incomprehensible how he lived at all – as an artist he had attained only the shadow of recognition", and if "all around us raged the recently victorious Cubism", this new current had remained quite alien to Modigliani, as would the works of Chagall, who "had already brought his enchanted Vitebsk to Paris".

Anna Akhmatova declares that at that time Modigliani "was crazy about Egypt" and "was engaged in sculpture". He "used to work in

"[Modigliani] came and sat next to me. I was struck by his distinction, by his radiance and the beauty of his eyes. He was at once very unassuming and very noble. How different he was in every gesture, even the way he shook hands (…). He had superb hands, they were very sure hands."

Lunia Czechowska

the courtyard below his studio; in the deserted cul-de-sac the tapping of his chisel was audible. The walls of his studio were hung with portraits of an unbelievable length (from floor to ceiling (…))" (Anna Akhmatova, 1964).

The change which the Russian poet had witnessed was a harbinger of what was to come in 1912. Max Jacob, his old friend Ortiz de Zárate and the illustrator Umberto Brunelleschi were worried about Modigliani's physical exhaustion and extreme nervous tension in those years. One torrid day in the summer of 1912, Ortiz de Zárate found Modigliani lying unconscious on the floor of his room. At that point the hat was passed round among his friends to raise the money for him to go back to his mother in Livorno.

In the autumn of 1912 Amedeo Modigliani came back to Paris laden with books by Petrarch, Dante, Ronsard, Baudelaire, Mallarmé and the comte de Lautréamont, pseudonym of Isidore Ducasse, whose *Les Chants de Maldoror* was very popular at the time. His return had been financed by his brother Umberto, and Modigliani showed seven of his sculptures at the Salon d'Automne. They were probably the sculptures that his Italian friend Gino Severini, who had been in Paris ever since Modigliani had arrived, had seen in a still rough-hewn state "in the midst of the plants (…) in the little garden" of his studio at the Cité Falguière, when with "that halting way he had of saying things" he had explained "I wanted to renew myself completely" (Gino Severini, 1948). The works of that moment were the fruit of "his curiosity", which in the last few years had ranged from the "forms created by the archaic Greeks" to "Khmer sculpture, which was beginning to come to the attention of painters and sculptors and assimilated many things", and "the refined art of the Far East", as well as "the simplified proportions of Negro sculptures" (S. Buisson, 1988), which he had been weighing up since the time of Rue du Delta.

That was the year of his liaison with one of his models, a thirty-year-old woman called Gaby. She was certainly not the first model with whom Modigliani had a relationship. In fact one of the earliest had been a woman whom Paul Alexandre described as very elegant, Maude Abrantes, who posed for several drawings and was immortalized by Modigliani in a canvas painted around 1907.

At that time, like other artists who later came together under the name of the "School of Paris", including Kisling, Kikoine, Vlaminck, Derain and Osterlind, Modigliani frequented the home of the police officer Eugène Descaves, who used to buy pictures from the young artists ten at a time, and who also sold them to another officer, Leon Zamaron, the man who was in the habit of freeing Modigliani and Utrillo from the police stations where they ended up after their recurrent and spectacular binges.

In 1914 Modigliani did everything he could to sell something, but needed a figure of reference, a mentor, a merchant, a collector who would be able to promote him.

And so Max Jacob introduced Modigliani to Paul Guillaume, a young man of twenty-three who had recently opened his first gallery in Rue Miromesnil, on the Rive Droite, in the quarter of the grand institutional galleries where no other young merchant would have dared set foot. Guillaume was certainly ambitious and had great success with the sale of African art, but as a hard-headed busi-

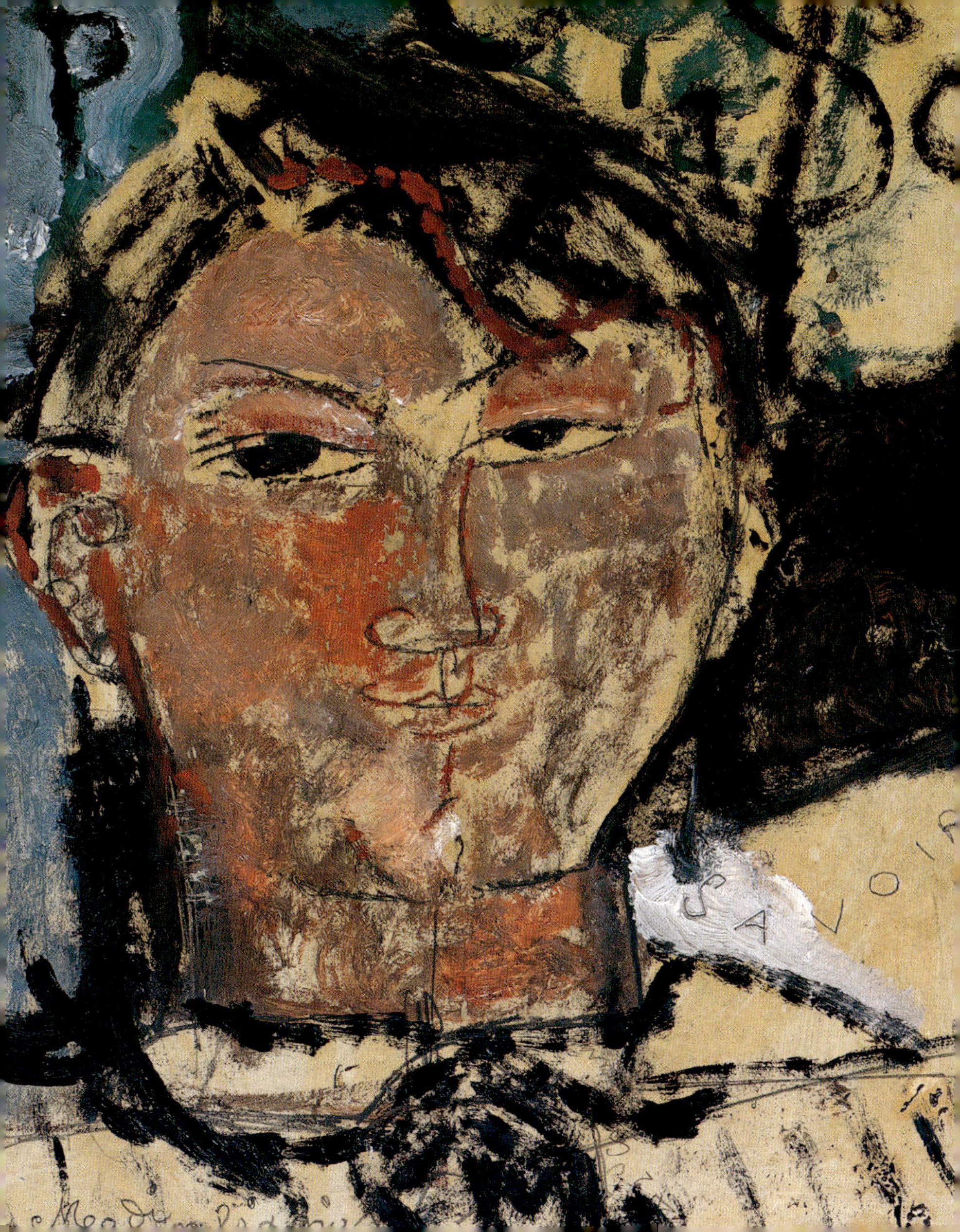
SAVOIR

nessman was not much interested in the artist himself, only in his production. This is probably why he urged Modigliani to devote himself to painting rather than sculpture, which was harder to sell, and then, as a shrewd dealer, went on paying Modigliani little for his works even though his profits were growing steadily. The partnership between the two men was not a particularly happy one and both may have been relieved when Leopold Zborowski came forward to offer the painter his first contract.

Of the time when he was responsible for promoting Modigliani, Guillaume recalled that "in 1914, throughout the year 1915 and for part of the year 1916, I had been Modigliani's only buyer and it was not until 1917 that Zborowski got involved (…). At that time he was living with Beatrice Hastings, working at her house, at the painter Haviland's or in a studio that I had rented for him at number 13, Rue Ravignan, or in a small house in Montmartre that he lived in with Beatrice Hastings and in which he painted my portrait", the one with the inscription "Novo Pilota" at the bottom.

Beatrice Hastings has entered legend as an eccentric, authoritarian and seductive figure. According to some she encouraged Modigliani to drink and take drugs, while others claim that she tried to rehabilitate him and get him to work. She was a cultured woman, a poet and journalist, and for about two years was Modigliani's constant partner, living with him in Rue Norvins. They had met for the first time in a dairy in 1914 and Beatrice had thought him "ugly, ferocious, greedy": perhaps he was drunk. The next day, however, he was at the Cafe Rotonde, shaved and with the *Songs of Maldoror* in his pocket, and had "raised his cap with a pretty gesture", inviting her to come and see his work, and she had been unable to resist. He was "of a regal beauty in his beige velvet jacket that, after many washings, had assumed a pearly tint, his blue check shirt washed every day and a carelessly tied scarf". Forty years later Roger Wild, Léopold Survage and Ossip Zadkine would recall him in the same way, more elegant even than Max Jacob, who used to go around in a top hat.

During the long hours he spent at the tables of the Café Rotonde he would draw portraits of all the people sitting nearby and often try to sell his drawings to the customers. He would introduce himself, "I'm Modigliani, a Jew, five francs" for a portrait. His natural talent for play-acting appears to have found expression in every aspect of his life: the shy young man of the Venice years and the early days in Paris seemed to have vanished and Picasso mischievously commented that "it's odd but you never see Modigliani drunk anywhere but at the corners of the Boulevard Montmartre and the Boulevard Raspail", where his outbursts of rage took on a theatrical quality. By now he was known and highly regarded, even if exclusively within the narrow circle of intellectuals and artists, and money was still in short supply.

Around 1915, the artists and poets who had not gone to war had moved *en masse* to Montparnasse, and one of the places where they hung out was at number 3, Rue Joseph Bara, where Jules Pascin, Moise Kisling, and Per Krohg had their studio. They regularly organized *soirées* in which poets and painters took part, including Derain, Utrillo, Modigliani and Soutine, along with others from La Ruche, like Chagall, Archipenko and Zadkine. It was probably on one of these winter evenings that Leopold Zborowski and Modigliani met for the first time. The Pole Zborows-

"Modigliani's style might seem easy to imitate, but this is a false impression. Each portrait is the result of deep meditation in front of the sitter. The fakes, however clever, are too empty or too crude, which ougth to give them away at first glance. Modigliani never painted without meaning."

Paul Alexandre

ki was already a well-known intellectual and poet. Filled with enthusiasm for the young Italian's works, Leopold Zborowski offered Modigliani a contract at the beginning of 1916. The arrangement was for him to receive fifteen francs a day along with canvases, paints and models, in exchange for the exclusive right to his production. Modigliani accepted and from then on Zborowski shared with him not only what had been agreed, but everything else too. Modigliani became his regular guest, first at the Hotel Sunny, in Boulevard du Port-Royal, where he painted the first portrait of Lunia Czechowska, the wife of Zborowski's childhood friend, and then, after July 1916, in the flat at number 3, Rue Joseph Bara, where Kisling, Pascin and Krohg also worked. Modigliani preferred to paint in the dining room, the largest room in Zborowski's home. It was here, between 1916 and 1917, that Modigliani executed the majority of his portraits and a series of nudes, and from 1916 to 1923 Utrillo and Soutine, who were working for Zborowski like Modigliani, used to come almost every day to the same apartment.

After relations with Beatrice Hastings had grown increasingly stormy, Modigliani and the journalist broke off their affair for good.

During the carnival celebrations of 1917, Modigliani met a young student at the Académie Colarossi called Jeanne Hébuterne, aged just nineteen. Roger Wild's wife, who knew her before she went to live with Modigliani, recalled her as a sober and intelligent girl with a strong personality.

In July 1917 Jeanne and Amedeo rented a studio at number 8, Rue de la Grande Chaumière. Leopold Zborowski hoped that a happy relationship would give Modigliani the energy to put his life in order. To encourage him, he organized an exhibition at Berthe Weill's gallery in the autumn of 1917. On the day of the exhibition's opening the nudes on display caused a scandal and the district commissioner of police, whose office was opposite the gallery, had to intervene, threatening to confiscate the paintings. Fortunately the exhibition was not closed, but Weill and Zborowski were only able to sell two drawings, at thirty francs each. So Berthe Weill, in order not to discourage Zborowski, bought five pictures.

In the meantime Modigliani went on working at an ever increasing pace, but his health was deteriorating and Jeanne was pregnant. Thinking to help the couple, Zborowski suggested they spend the winter in the South of France. Anna and Leopold Zborowski, Amedeo, Jeanne and her mother all left together. In the Midi Modigliani lightened his palette and worked on pictures of a larger size, while Zborowski provided him with an income of around five hundred francs a month.

On 29 November 1918 a baby girl was born at the maternity hospital in Nice. She was registered under the same name as her mother, Jeanne Hébuterne. Before leaving Nice, Zborowski had placed Modigliani in the charge of his friend the painter Osterlind. Osterlind had been living for years in the area with his wife Rachel, "the beautiful Rachel with golden eyes" (Jeanne Modigliani, 1958) who was dying of tuberculosis after succumbing to Spanish flu. Modigliani painted her sitting on a rocking chair with her head resting listlessly on her right hand, in the same pose in which we see her in a photograph that has the portrait in the background, propped up on the mantelpiece of the fireplace.

From a document in the police headquarters at Cagnes we know that Modigliani was back in Paris by 31 May 1919. Jeanne and their daughter did not arrive until a month later, and then Jeanne went back to the South, expecting another child from him.

Modigliani was starting to become a well-known painter, highly regarded by his colleagues, as Lipchitz and Douglas recalled, arguing that he would have been able to sell more pictures if he had not had such a difficult character.

He was even beginning to attract attention outside his Parisian entourage. In 1919 Zborowski had organized an exhibition in London which included ten of Modigliani's works, and the British critics Earp and Atkin supported his production enthusiastically. In the August of 1919 the painter wrote to his mother to tell her about his recent successes, but at the same time he was being consumed by the illness that was to kill him before long. A roll of drawings found by his brother Emanuele in the studio after his death showed that he had gone on drawing untiringly, portraits and above all nudes.

One day in January 1920, Kisling and Ortiz de Zárate found Modigliani in bed, in his icy studio in Rue de la Grande Chaumière. Alongside him, nine months pregnant, lay Jeanne Hébuterne, and around them there were pieces of coal, empty bottles of wine and open tins of sardines. He was taken to hospital, where he died in the evening of 24 January 1920, surrounded by his closest friends. That night, the provident Zborowski did not want Jeanne to go back to sleep in Rue de la Grande Chaumière and took her to a small hotel instead. "She seemed calm", declared her friend Paulette who accompanied her. The next day she went back to see Amedeo with her father, but "remained at the door", "did not kiss him" and "looked at him for a long time, without saying anything". During the day Jeanne Hébuterne returned to the Zborowskis and then allowed herself to be persuaded by her father and followed him to the family home in Rue Amyot. After several attempts, Jeanne Hébuterne jumped out of the fifth-floor window at four o'clock on the second night after Modigliani's death. "This girl, so full of talent, so absolute in her love for Modigliani", died instantly (C. Quenneville, 1958).

The legend was born. The stories and fantasies created a thick smokescreen around the figure of Amedeo Modigliani and people began to forge his works at once, leading to a great deal of confusion about his artistic production as well. Only in the last few decades have time and the work of many scholars stripped away the numerous anecdotes and identified a corpus of works that we can be certain are his and that seem wholly in keeping with the key to this personality provided a long time ago by another painter who knew him, and who like him lived those years to the full. Maurice de Vlaminck, the Fauve, wrote: "Modigliani was an aristocrat. His entire work is a powerful testimony to this. His canvases are all marked by a great distinction. The coarse, the banal, the vulgar are excluded from them" (S. Buisson and F. Fergonzi, 1988).

Works

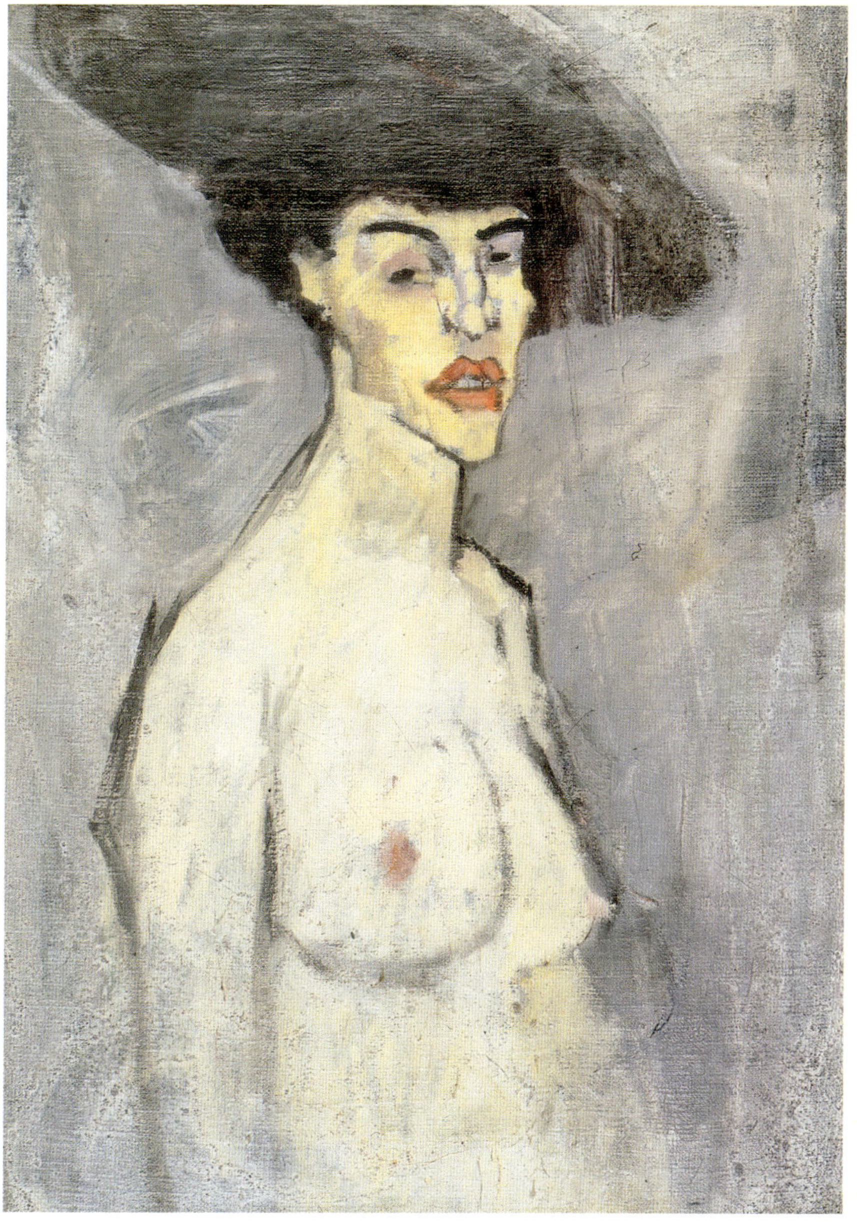

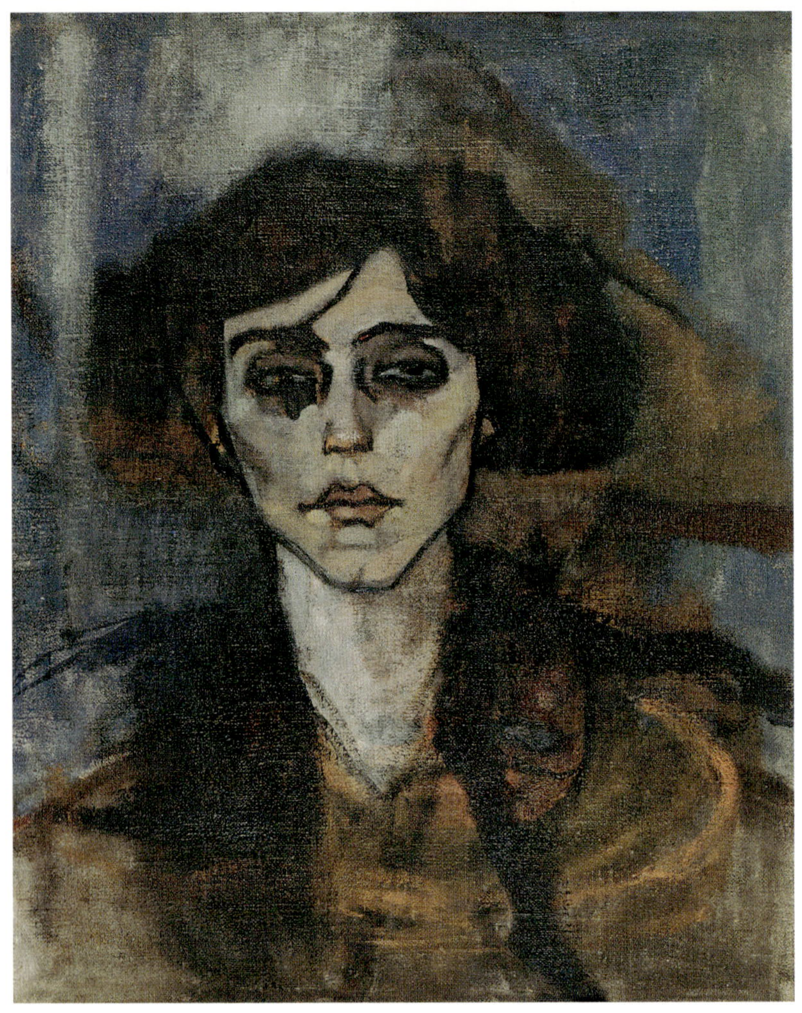

On page 35
1. *Bust of a Nude Woman*
(front), 1907-08

2. *Bust of a Nude Woman*
(back): *Maud Abrantes,*
1907-08

3. *Maurice Drouard*, 1909

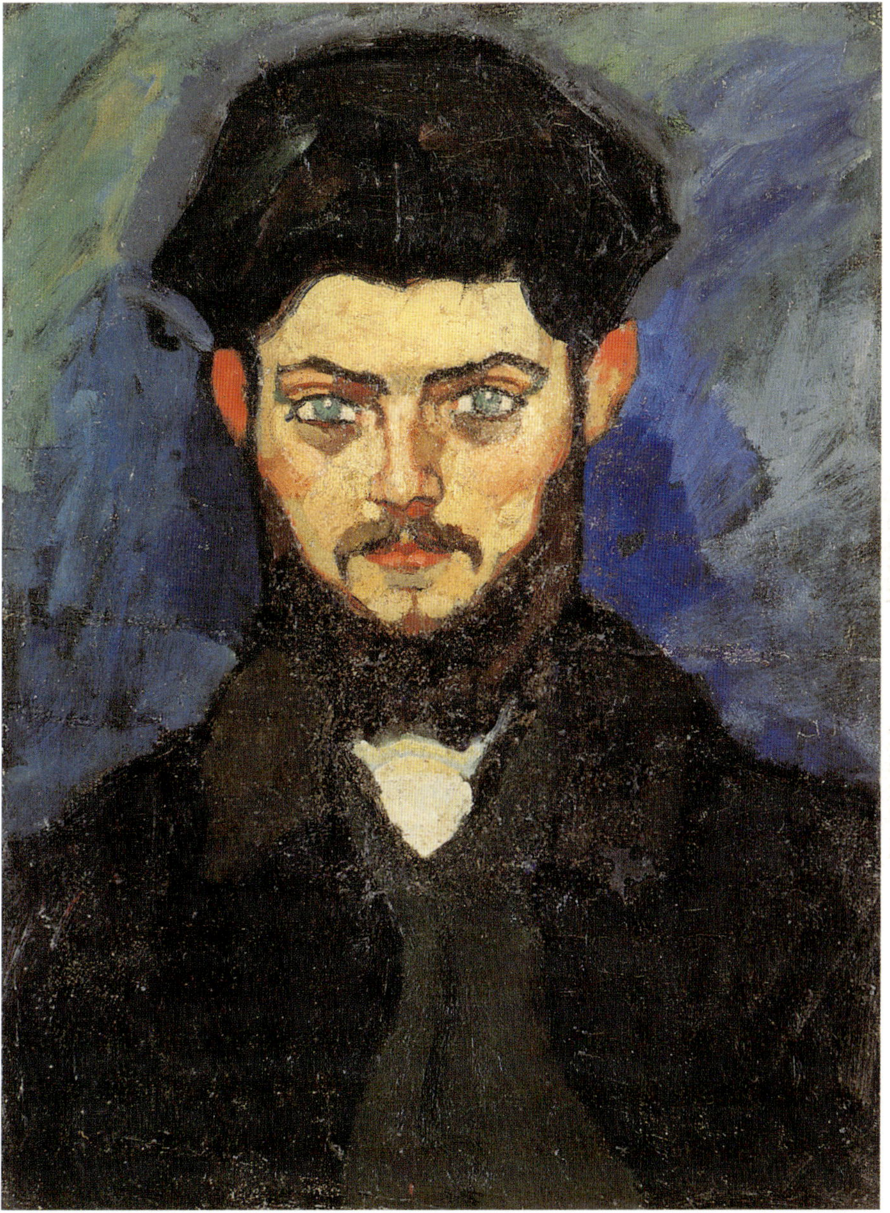

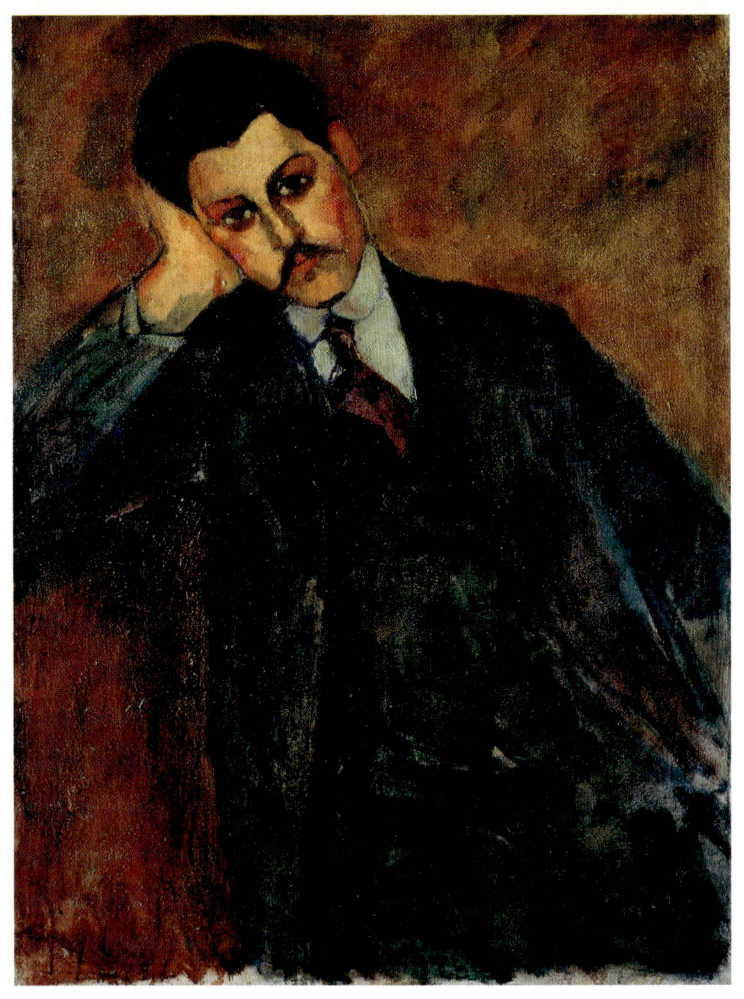

4. *Jean Alexandre*
(front), 1909

5. *Jean Alexandre* (back):
Seated Nude, 1909

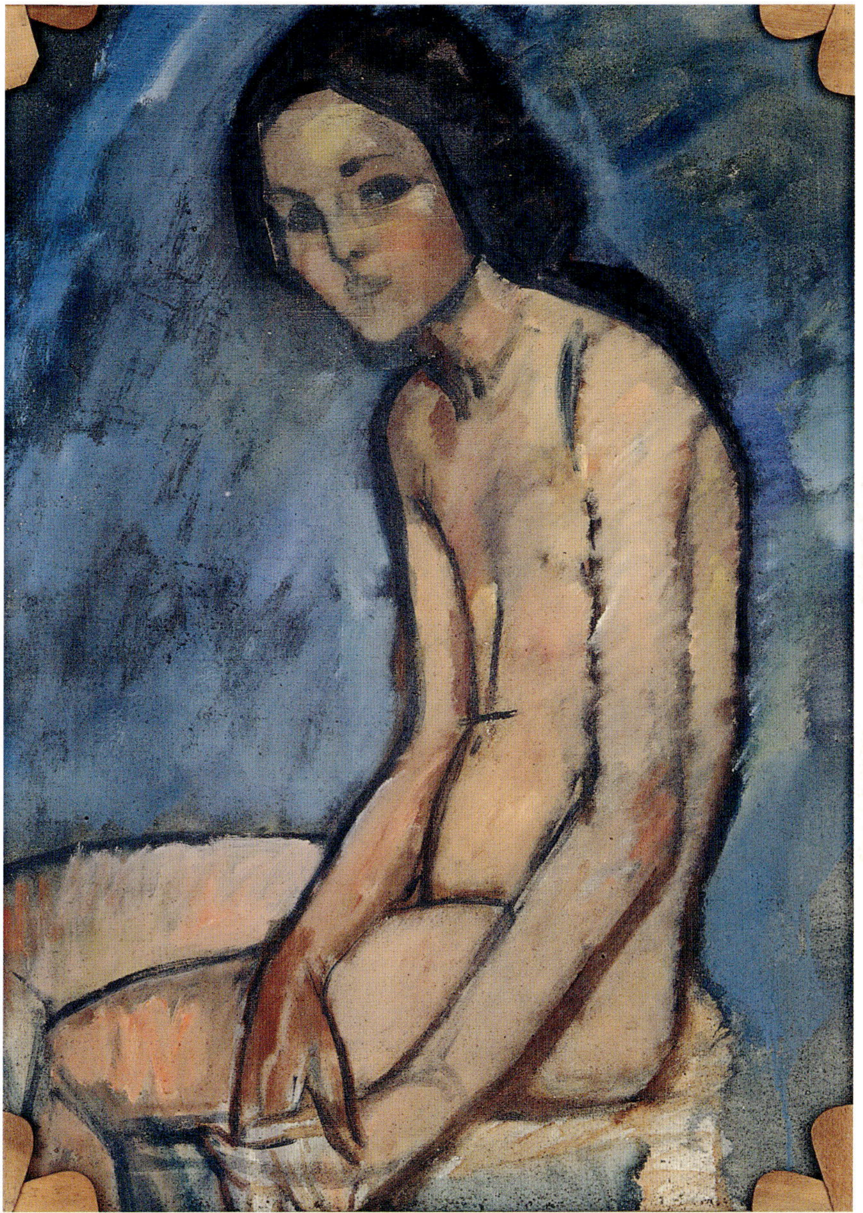

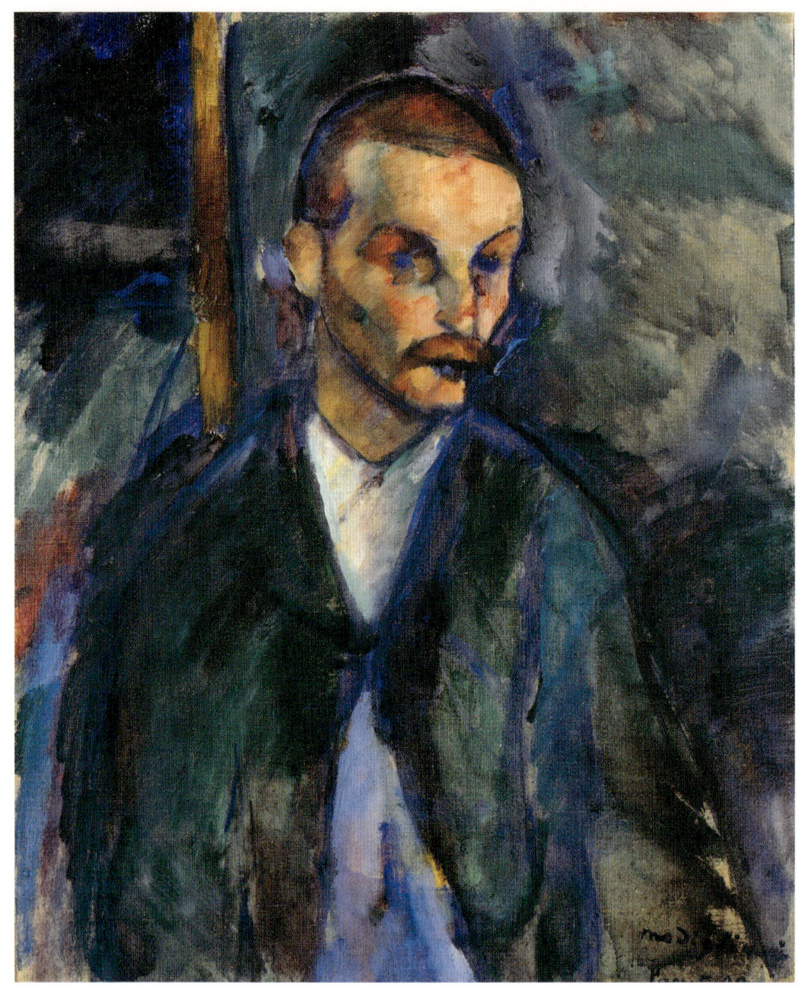

6. *The Beggar of Livorno,*
1909

7. *The Beggar,* 1909

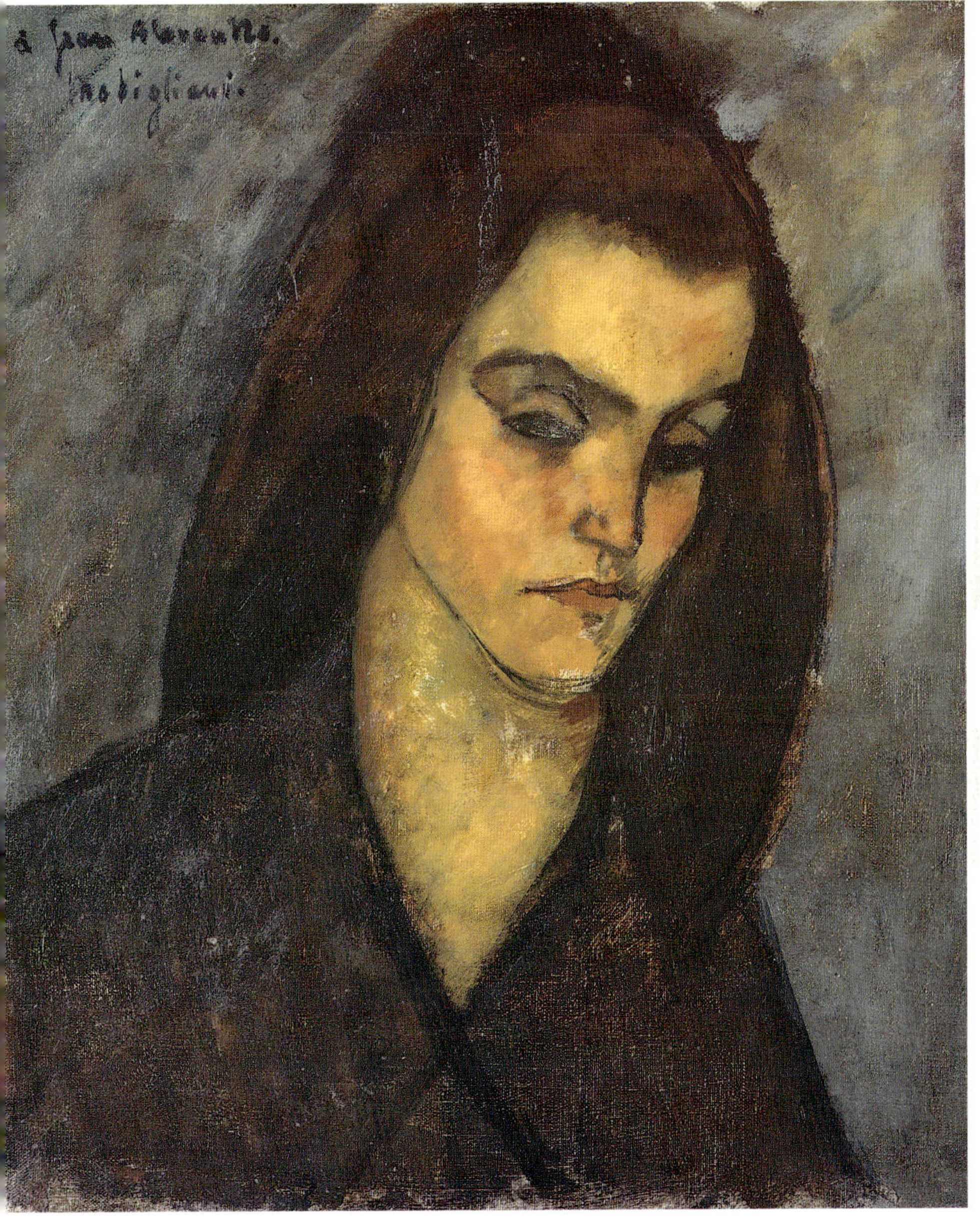

à Jean Alexandre.
Modigliani.

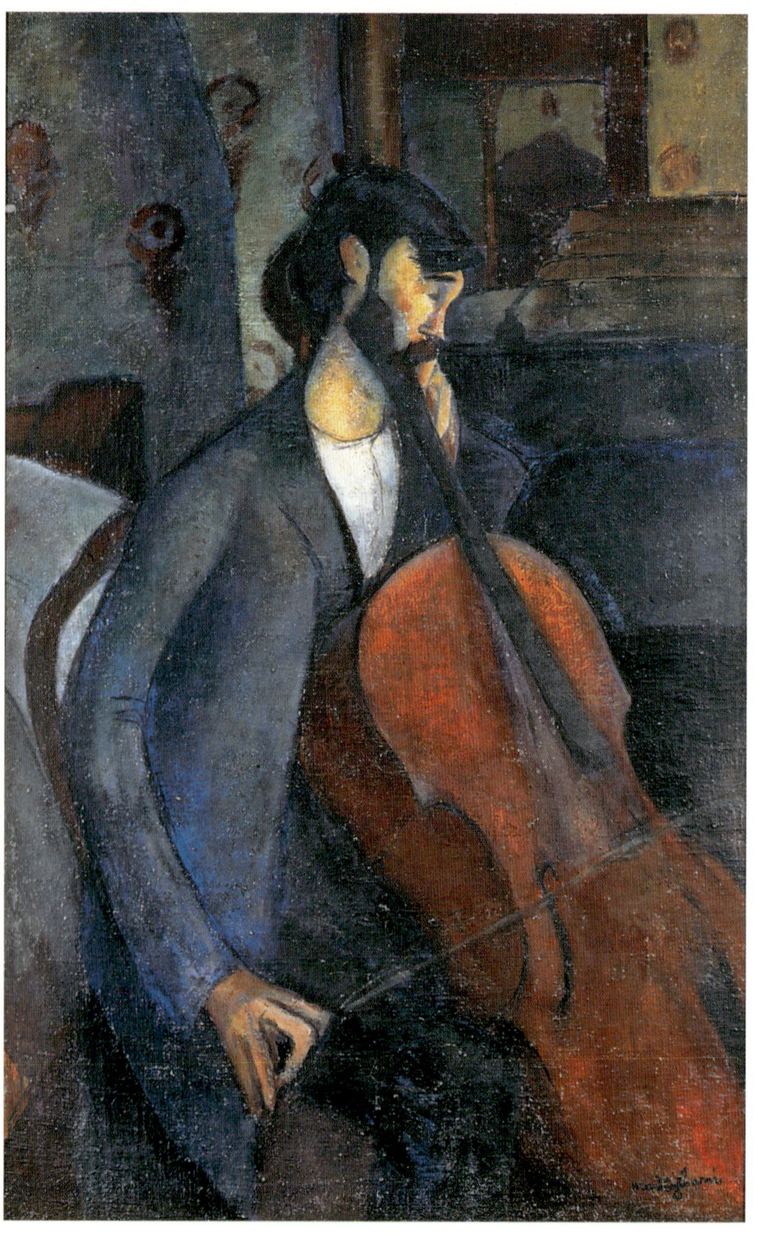

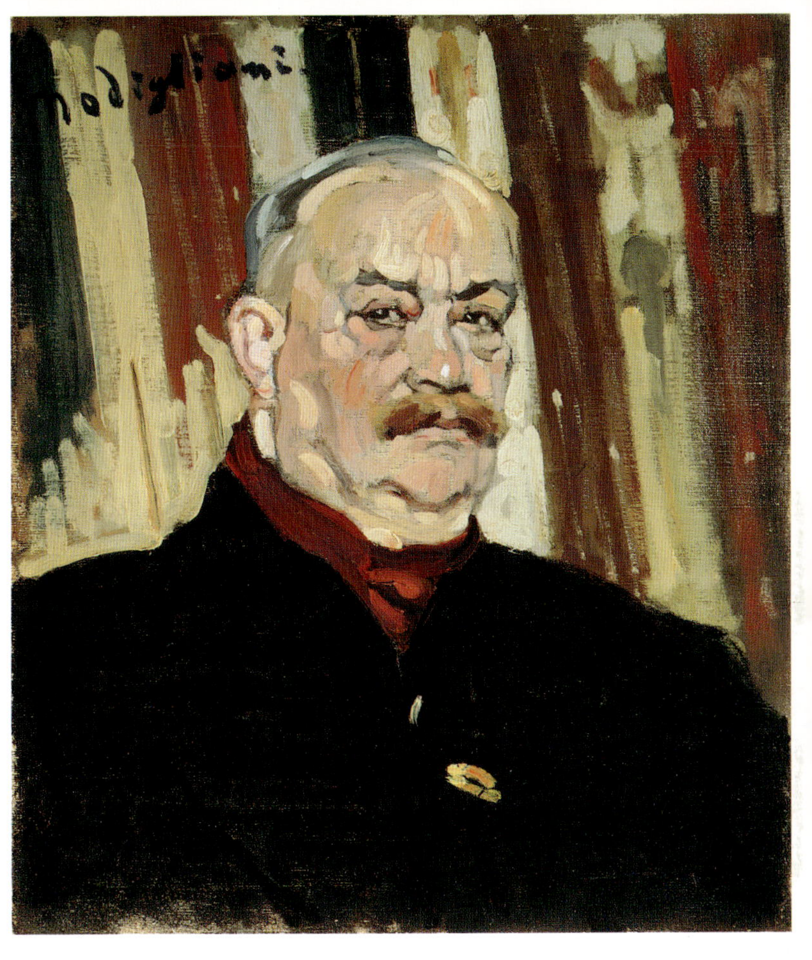

8. *The Cellist*, 1909

9. *Joseph Lévi*, 1910

43

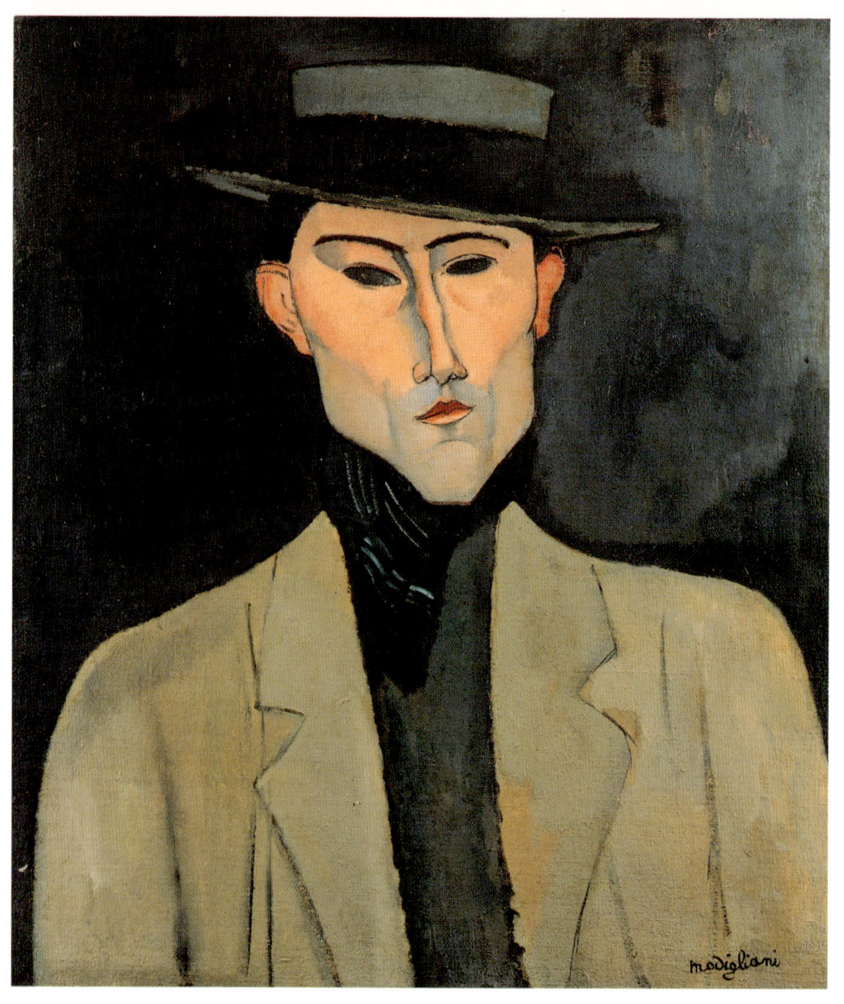

10. *Portrait of a Man with Hat (José Pacheco?),* 1910-11

11. *Bust of a Young Woman,* 1911

44

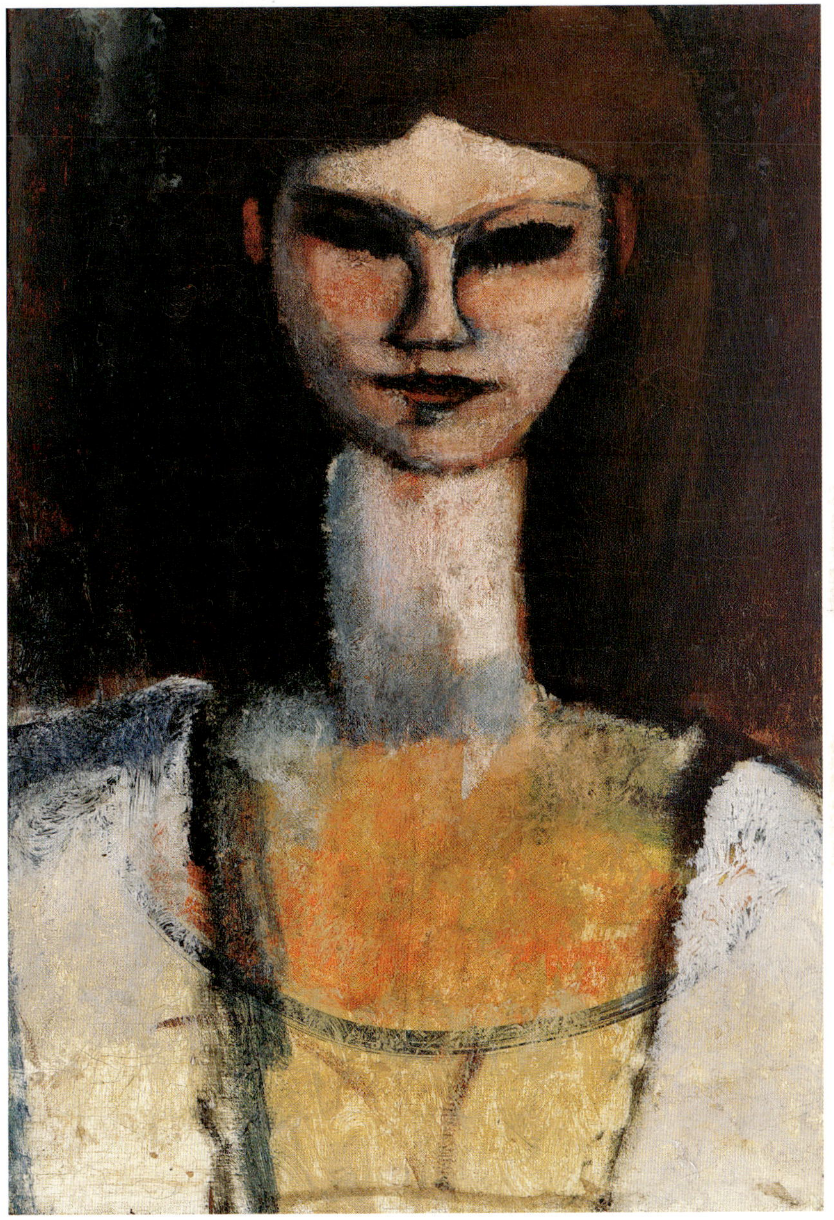

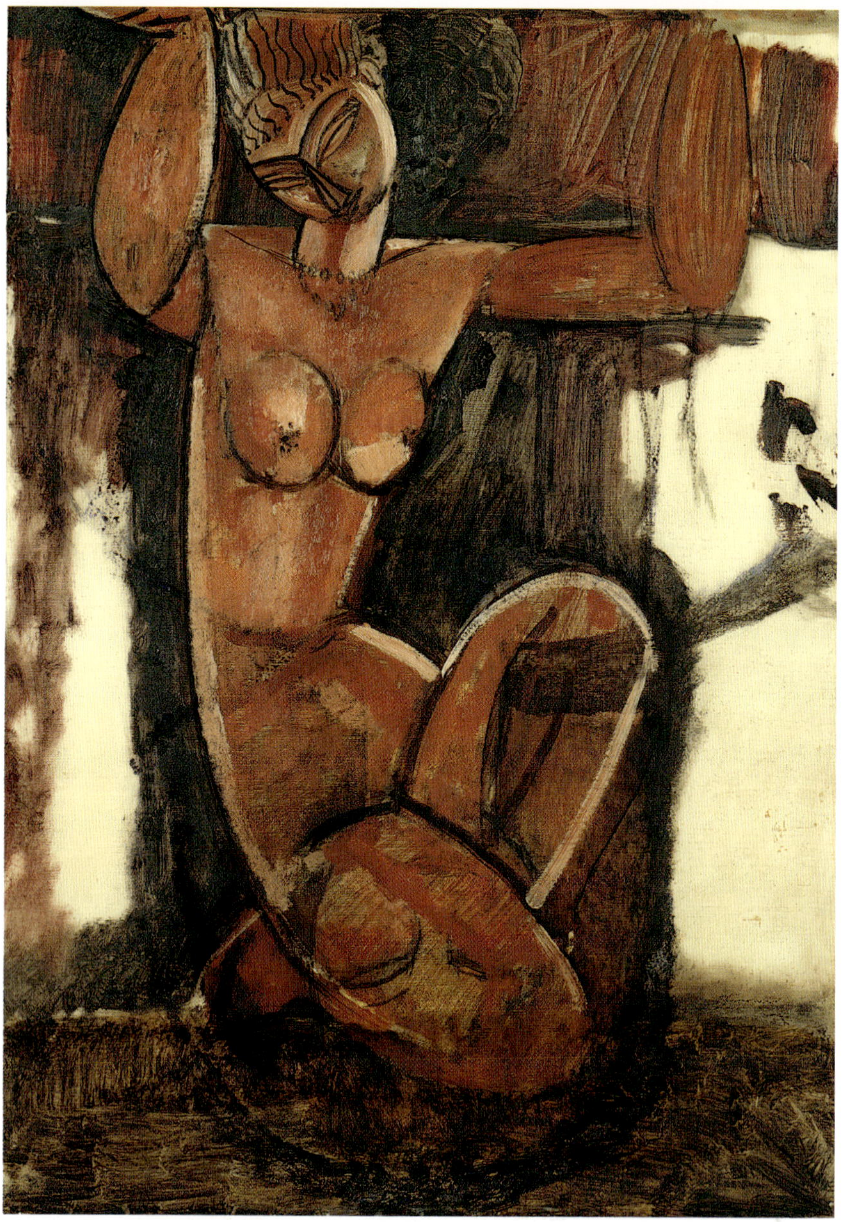

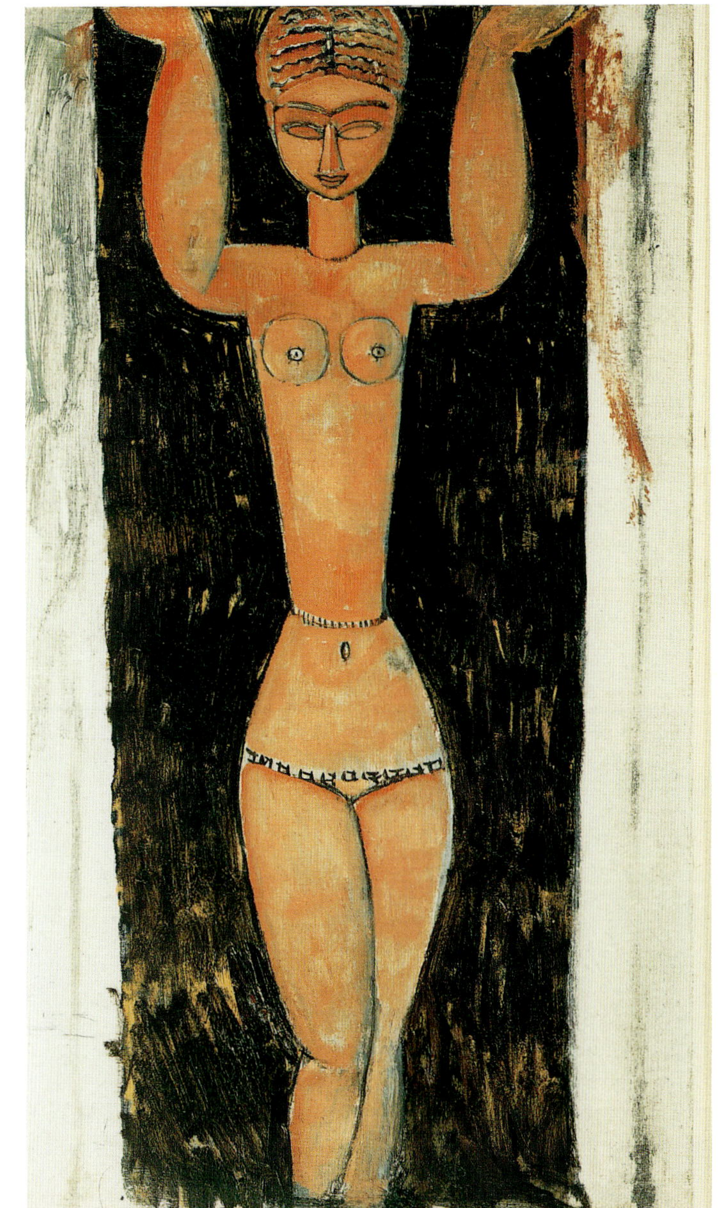

12. *Caryatid*
(*Mademoiselle Grain
de Café*), 1911-12

13. *Caryatid*, 1913

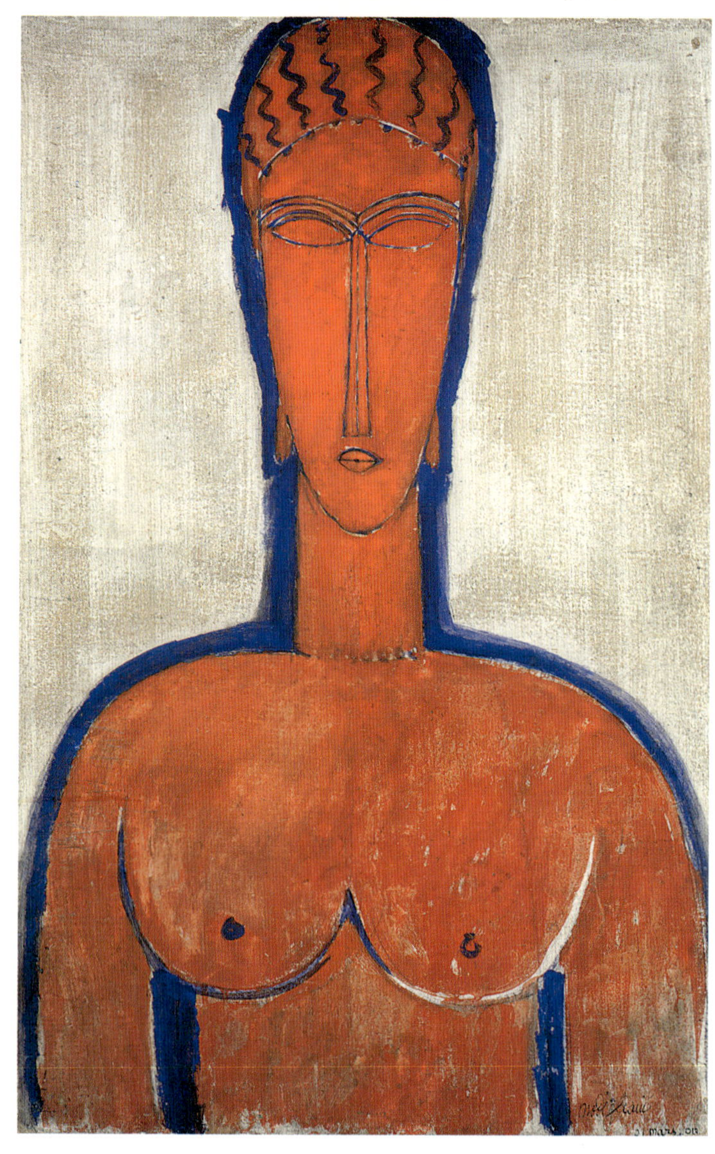

14. *Big Red Bust,* 1913

15. *Beatrice Hastings,* 1914

Following pages
16. *Head of a Woman,* 1915

17. *Head of a Woman with Red Hair,* 1915

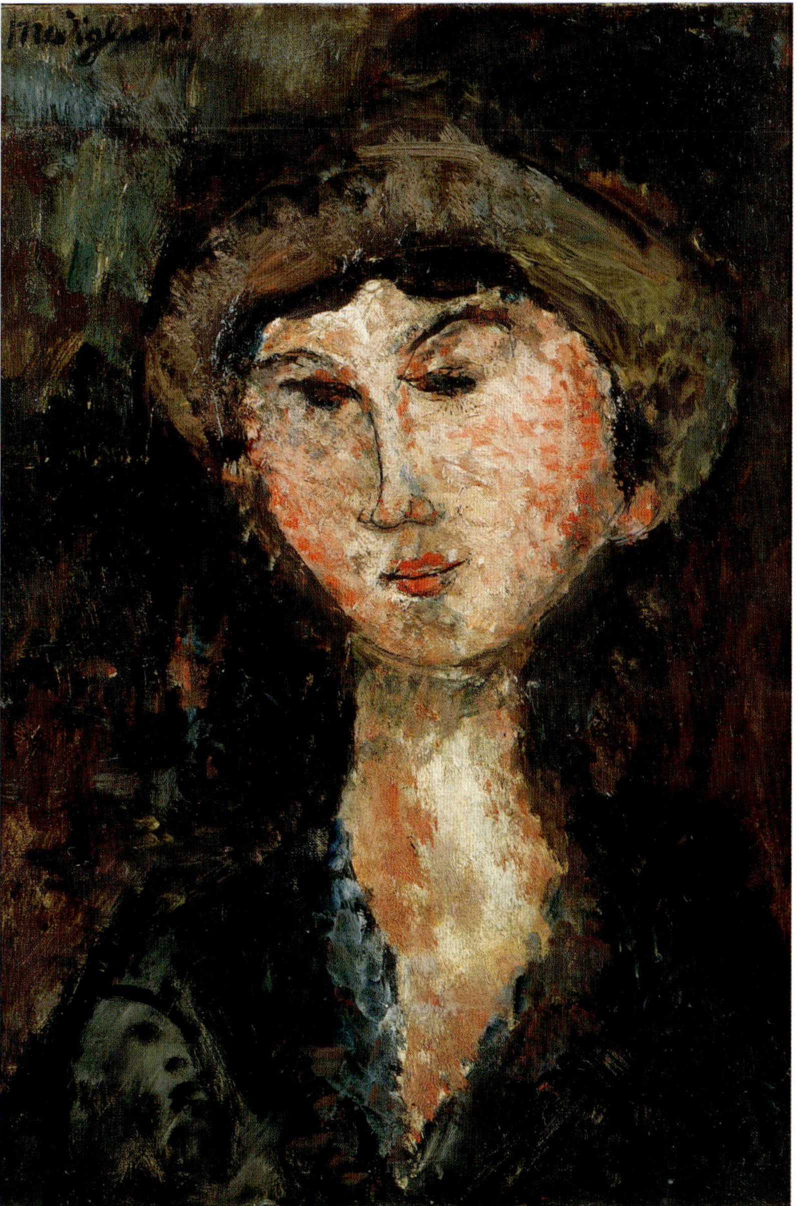

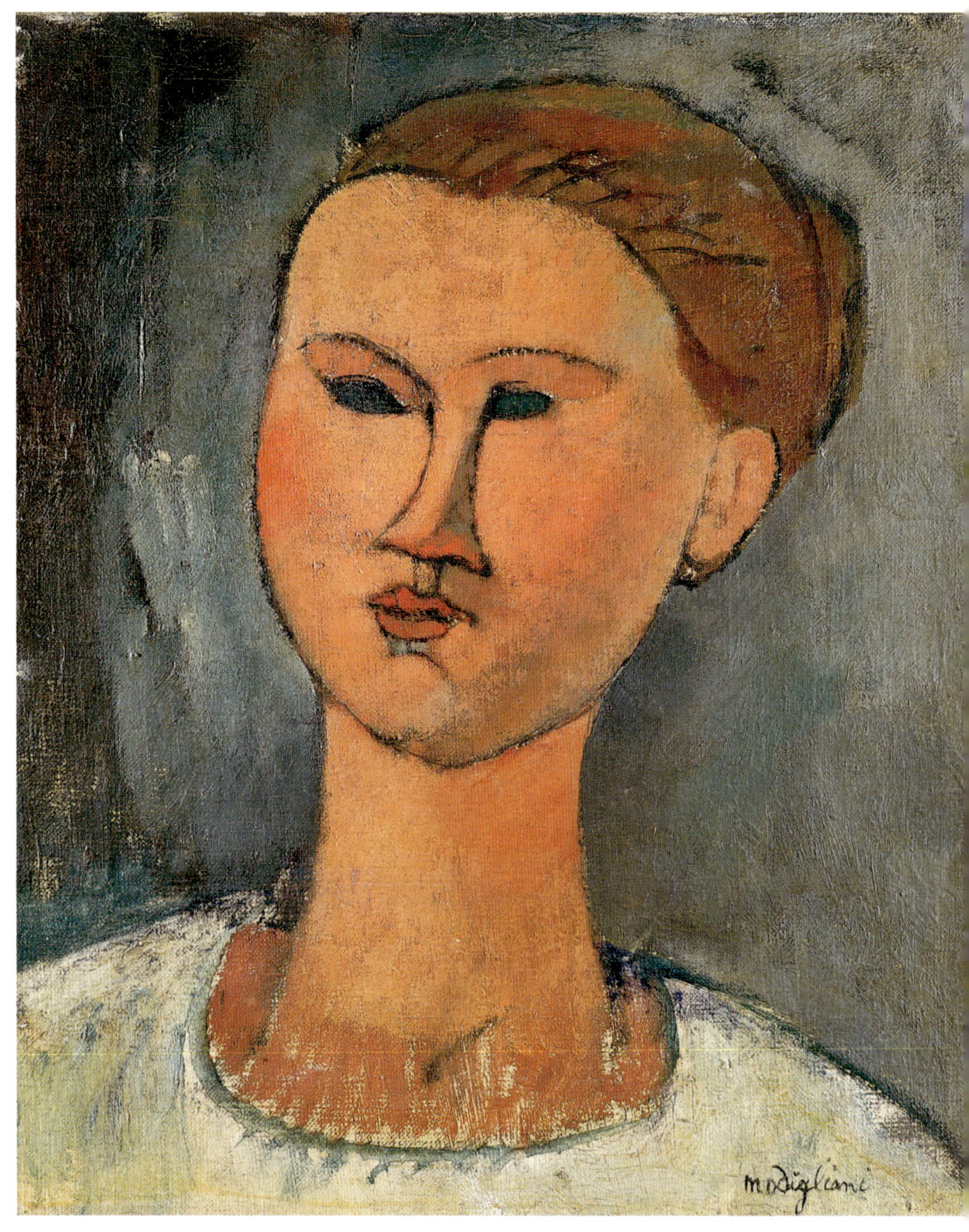

moDigliani

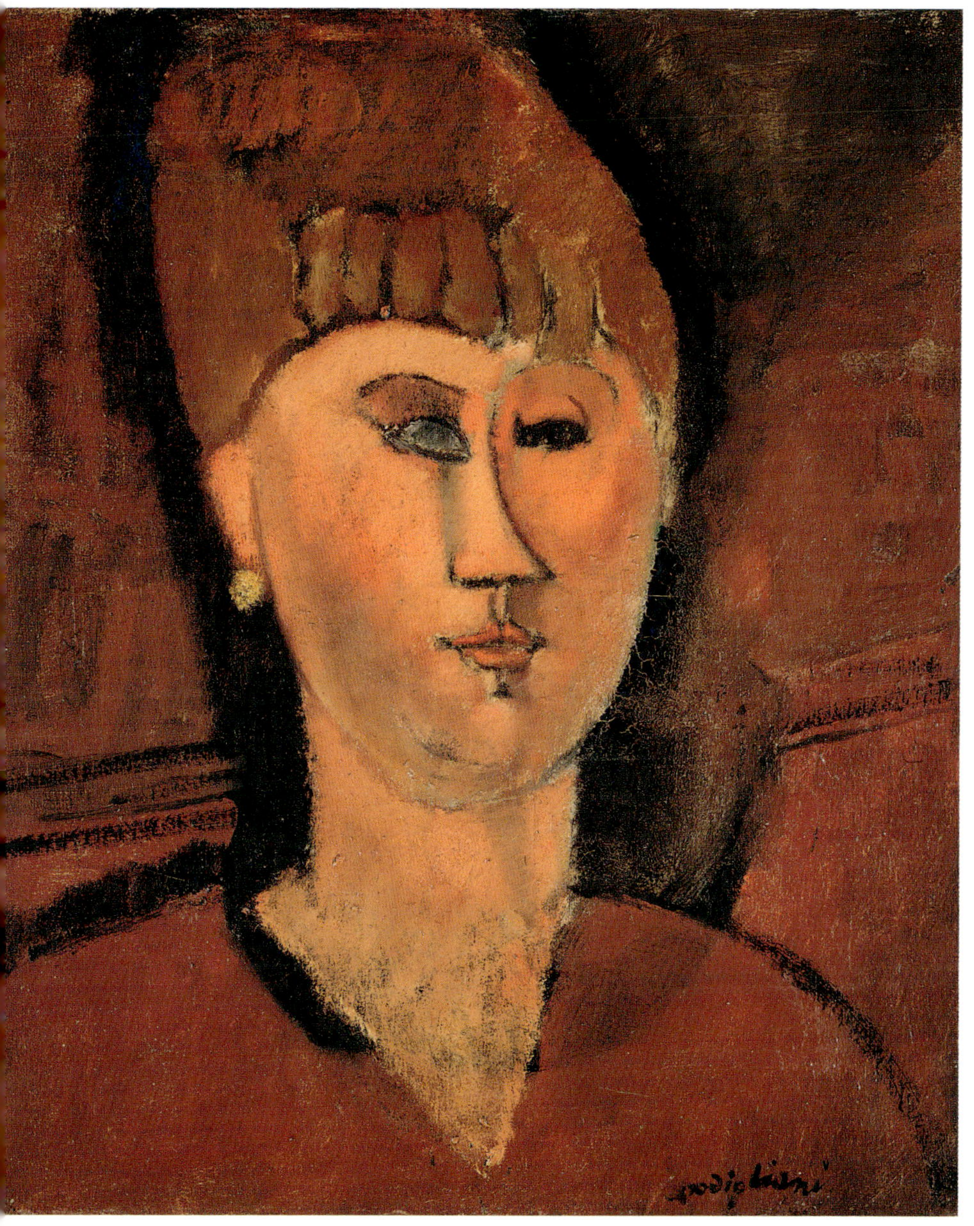

modigliani

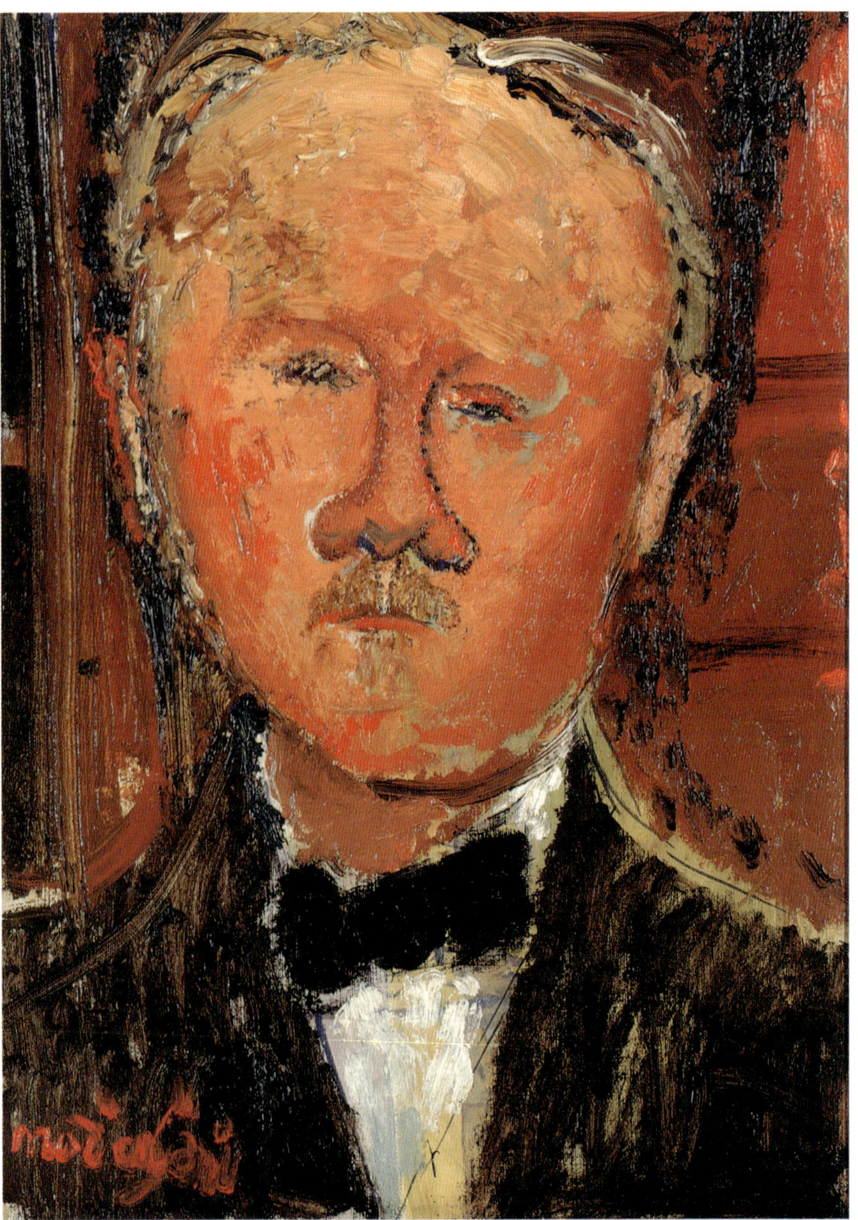

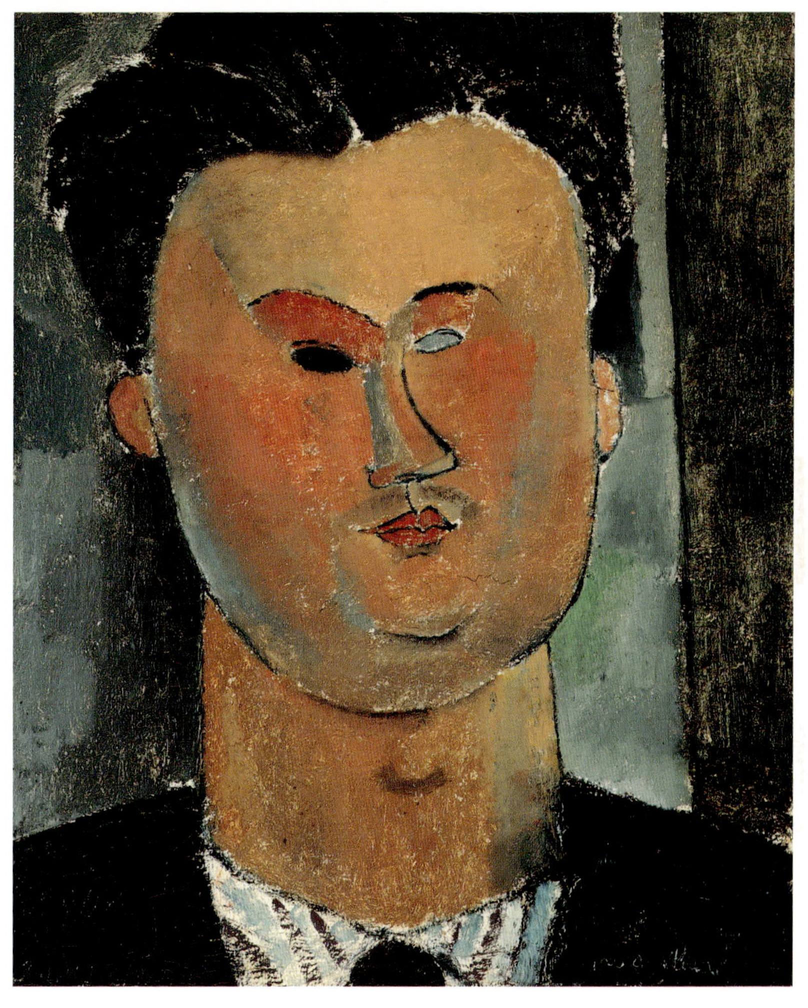

18. *Chéron*, 1915

19. *Pierre Reverdy*, 1915

53

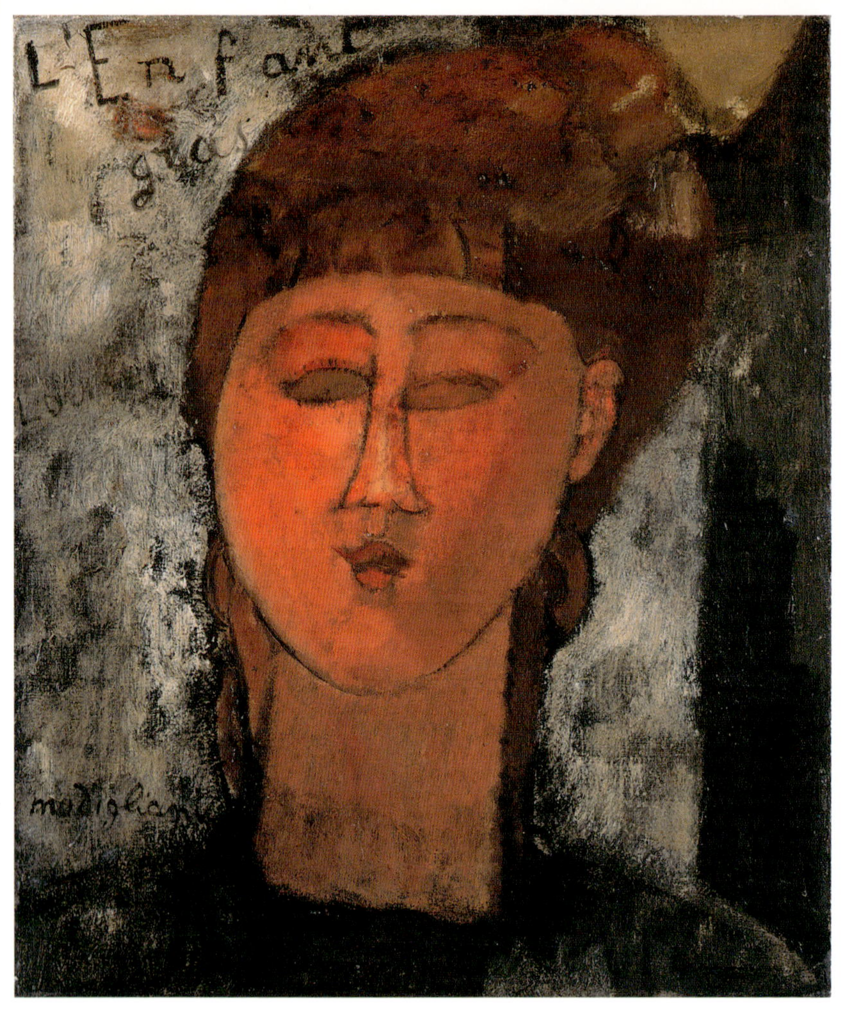

20. *L'enfant gras*
(*The Fat Child*), 1915

21. *Raimondo*, 1915

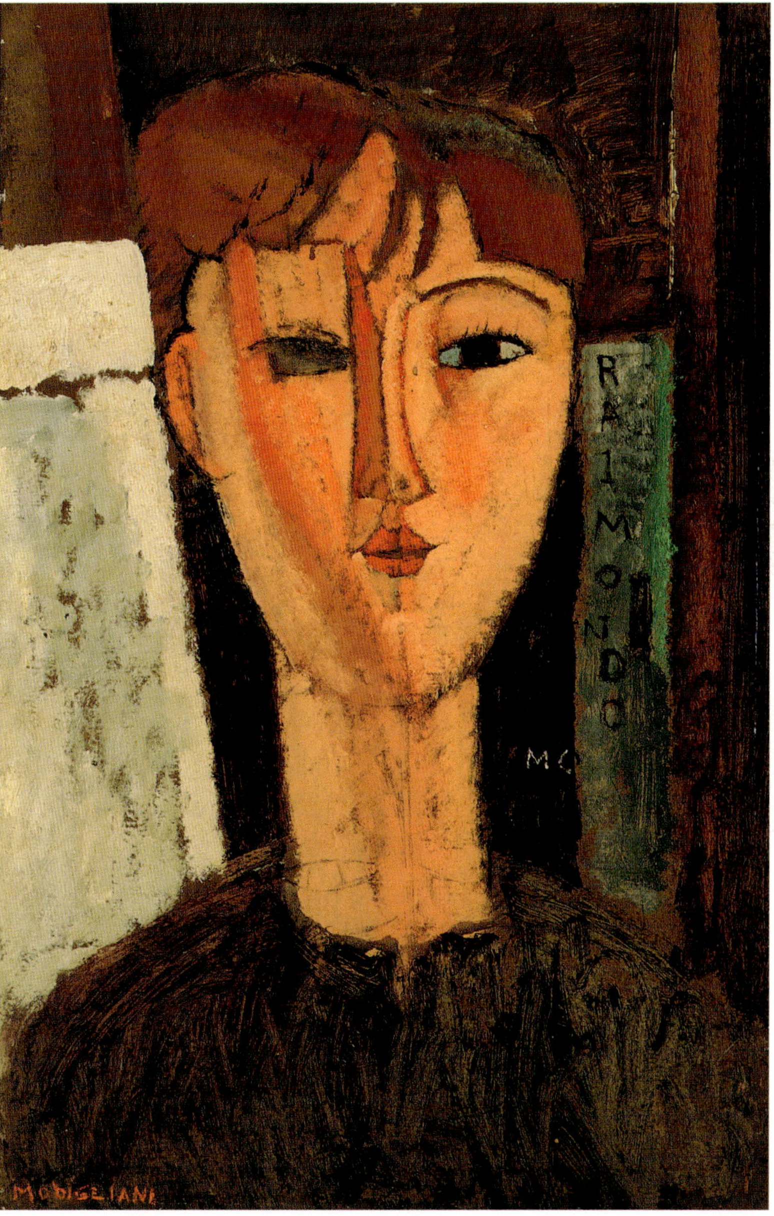
RA
1M
O
ND
O
MODIGLIANI

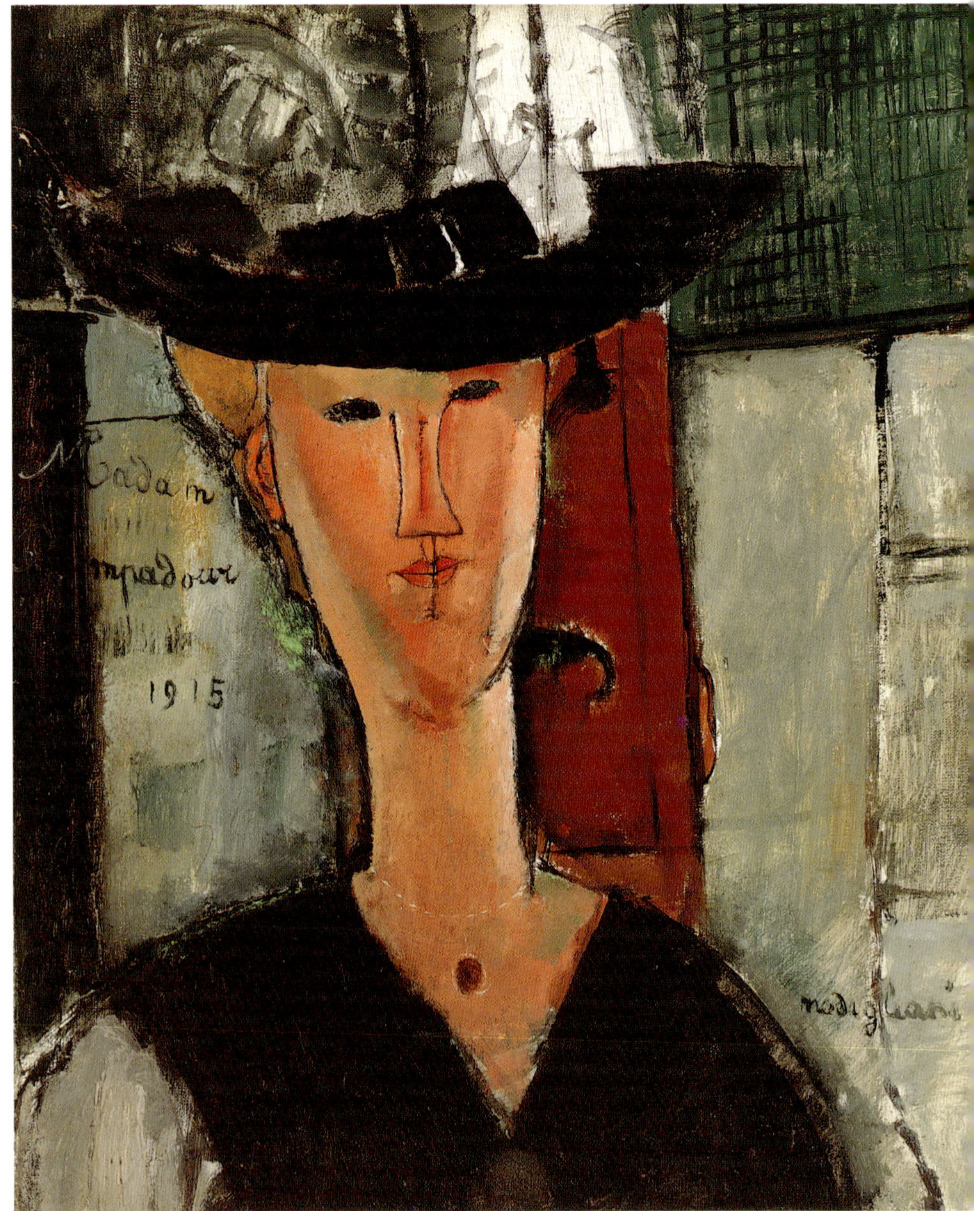

Madam
mpadour
1915
modigliani

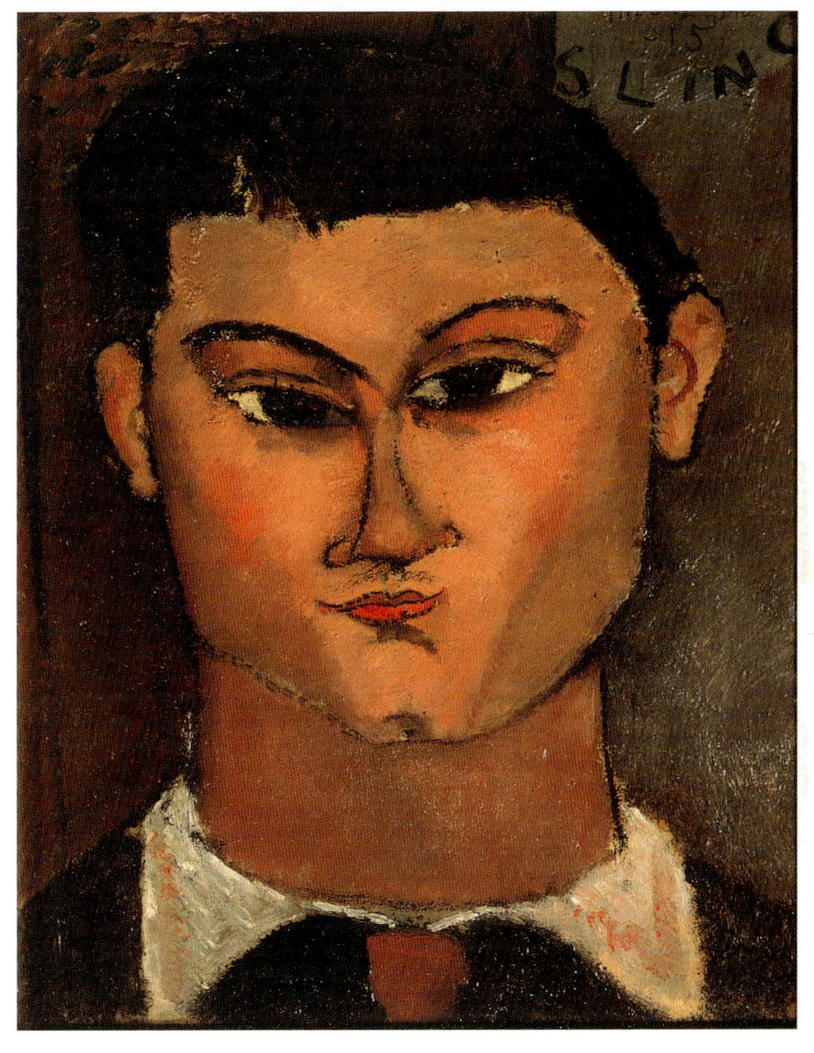

22. *Madam Pompadour (Portrait of Beatrice Hastings), 1915*

23. *Moïse Kisling, 1915*

57

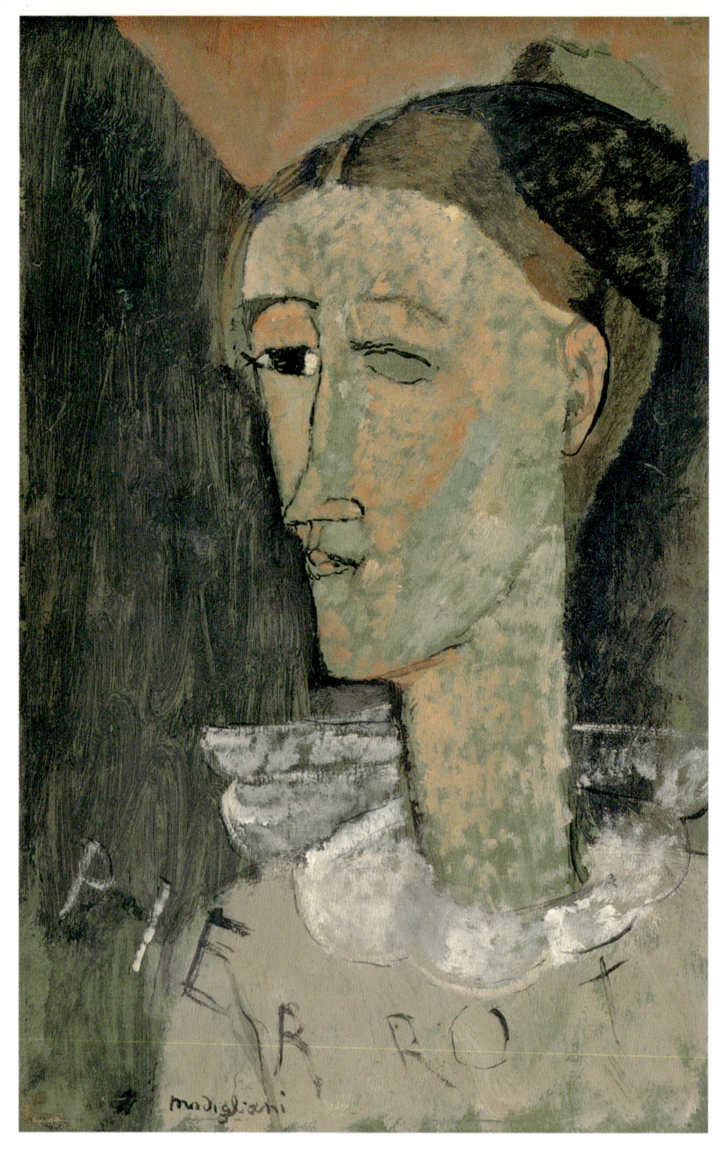

24. *Pierrot (Self-Portrait in Pierrot Costume)*, 1915

25. *Head of a Woman with Velvet Ribbon (The Black Border)*, 1915

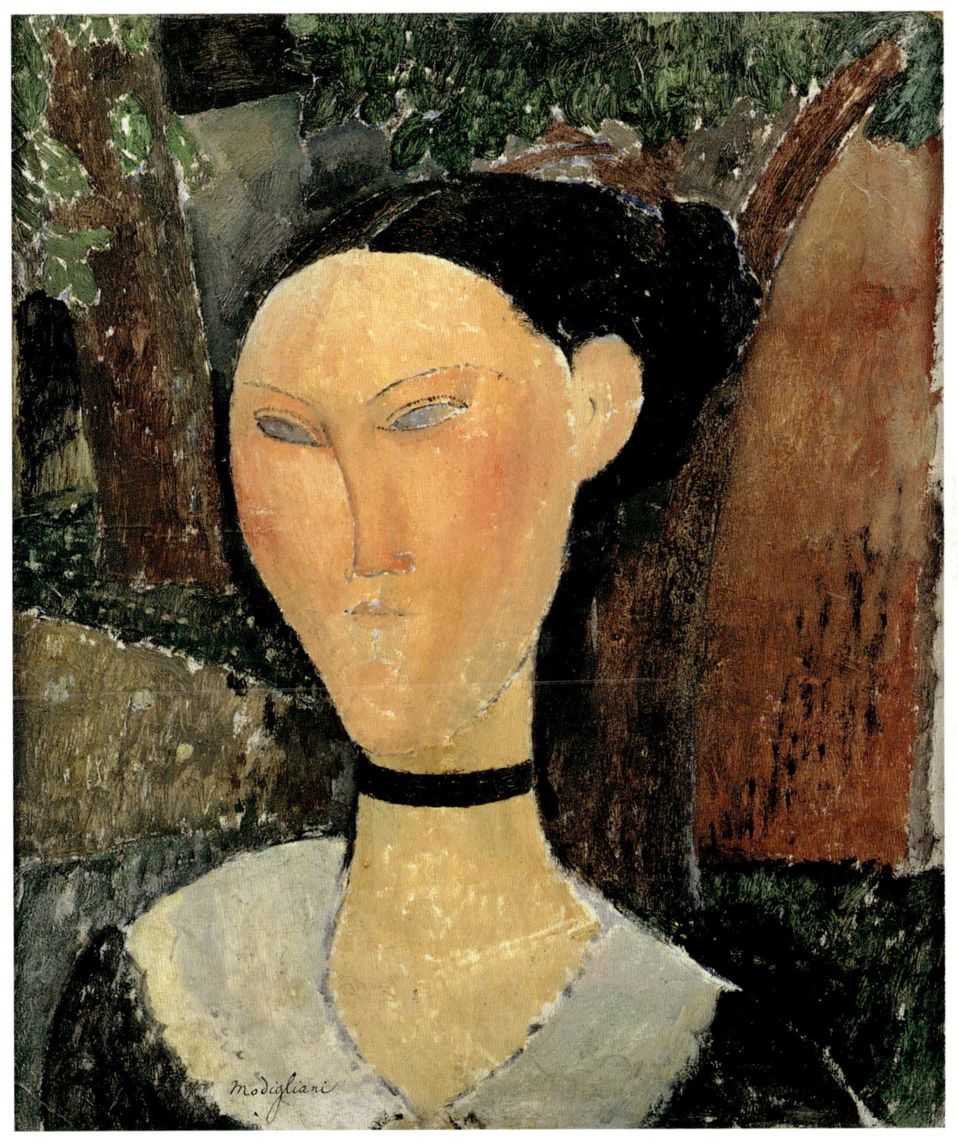

59

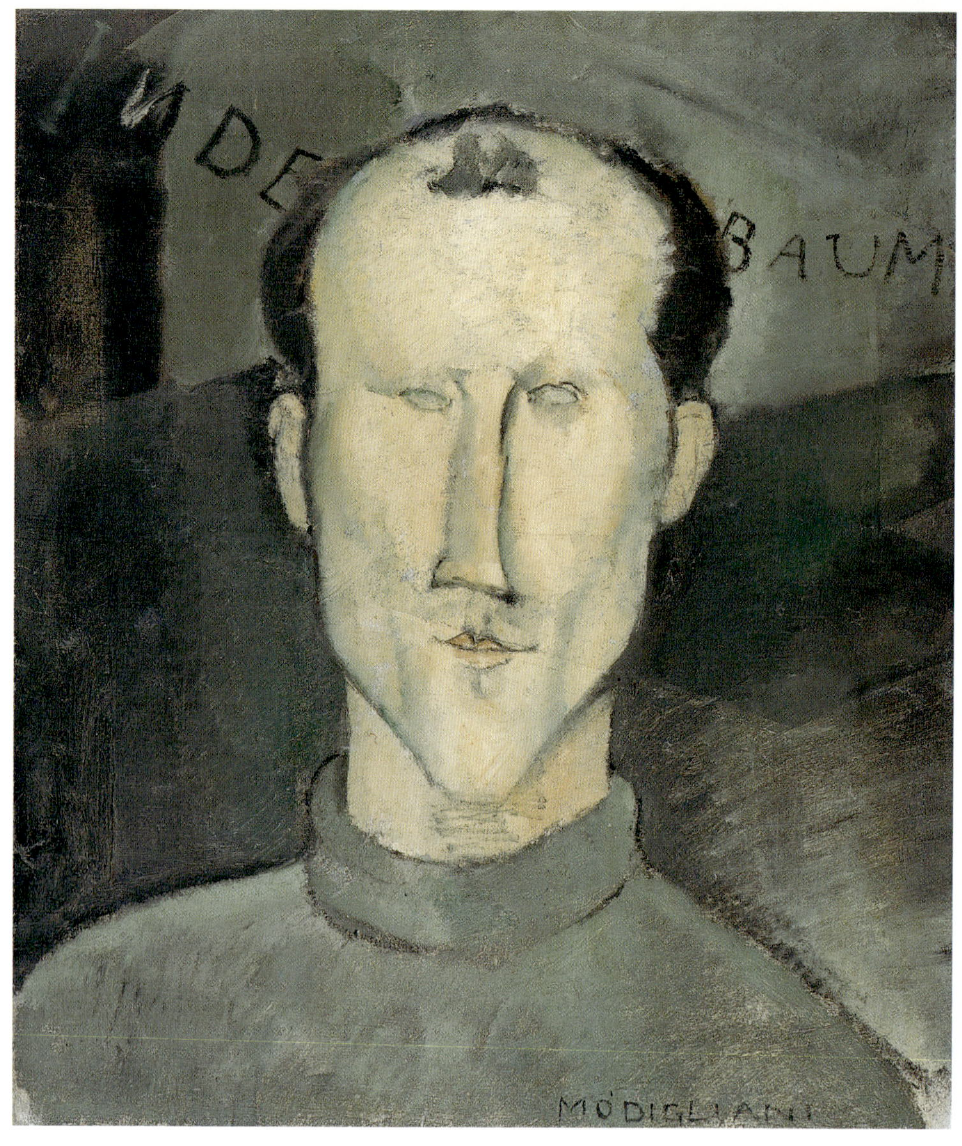

IN DE
BAUM
MODIGLIANI

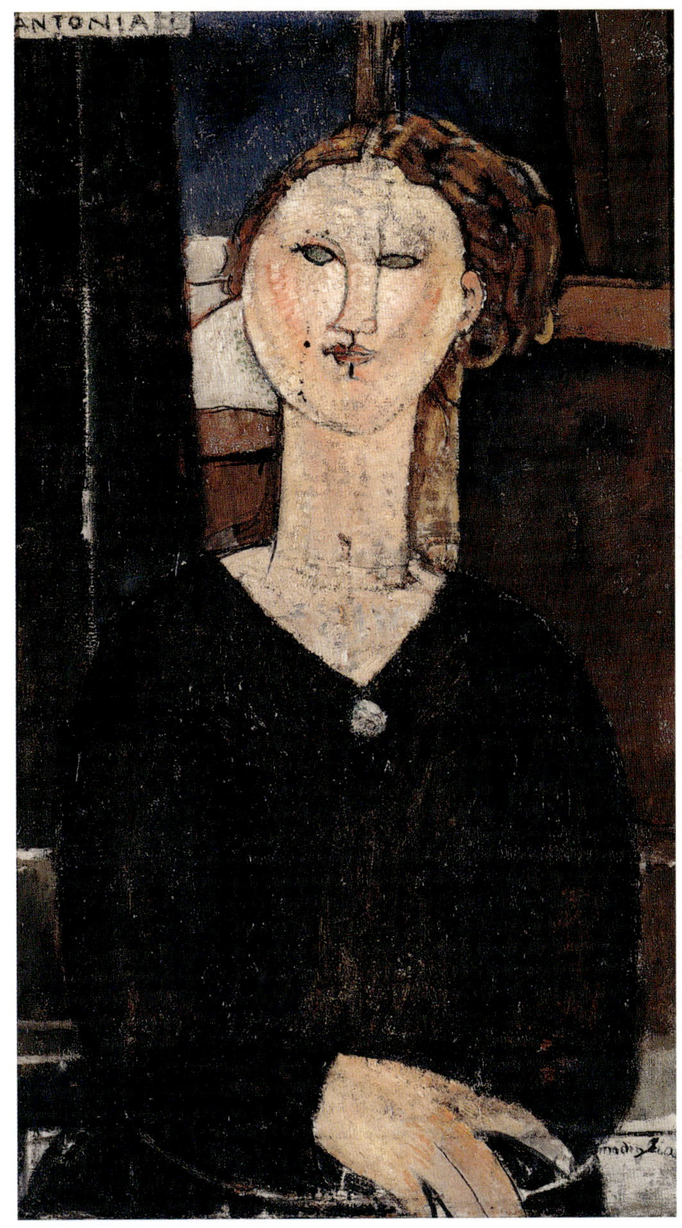

26. *Léon Indenbaum*, 1915

27. *Antonia*, 1915

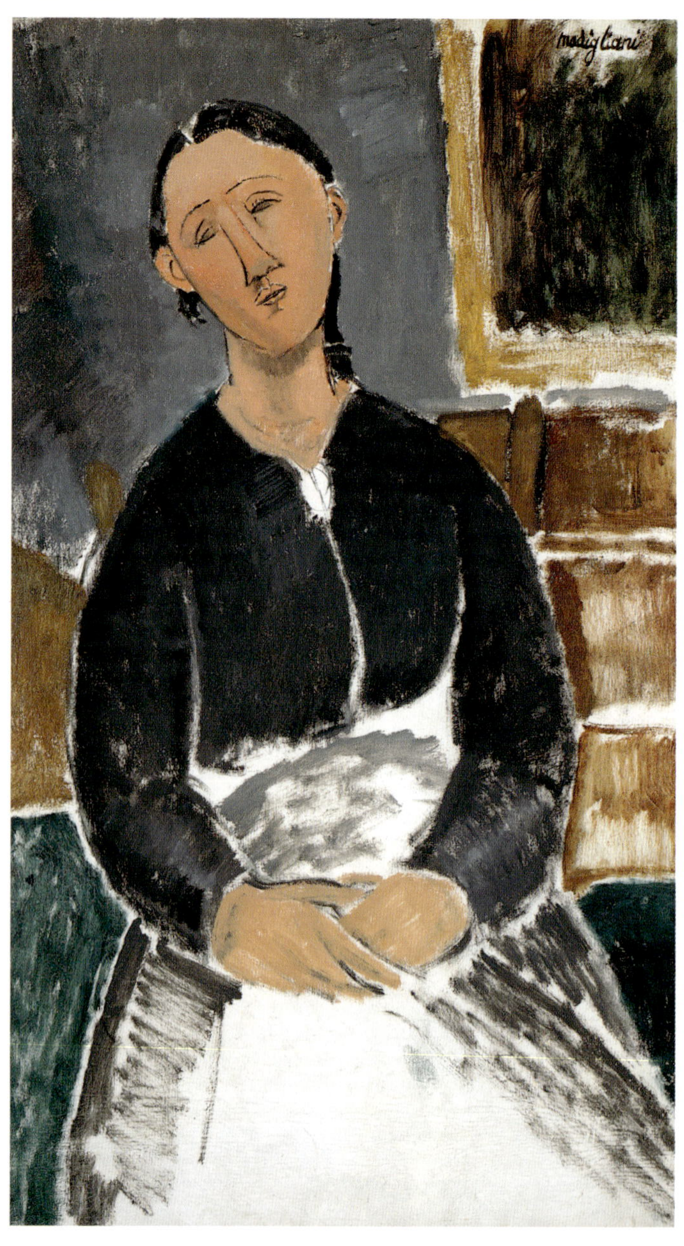

28. *The Maid*, 1915

29. *Paul Guillaume Seated*, 1916

Following pages
30. *Manuel Humbert Estève*, 1916

31. *Léopold Zborowski*, 1916

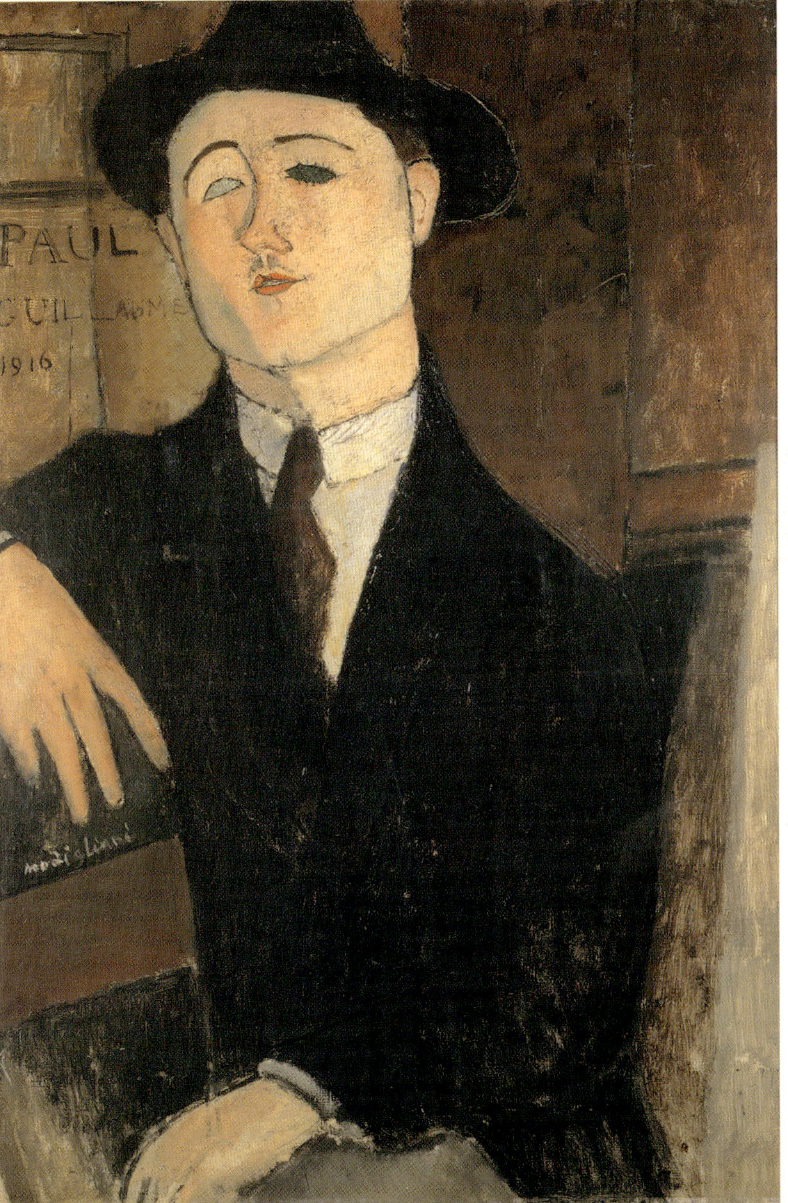
PAUL
GUILLAUME
1916
modigliani

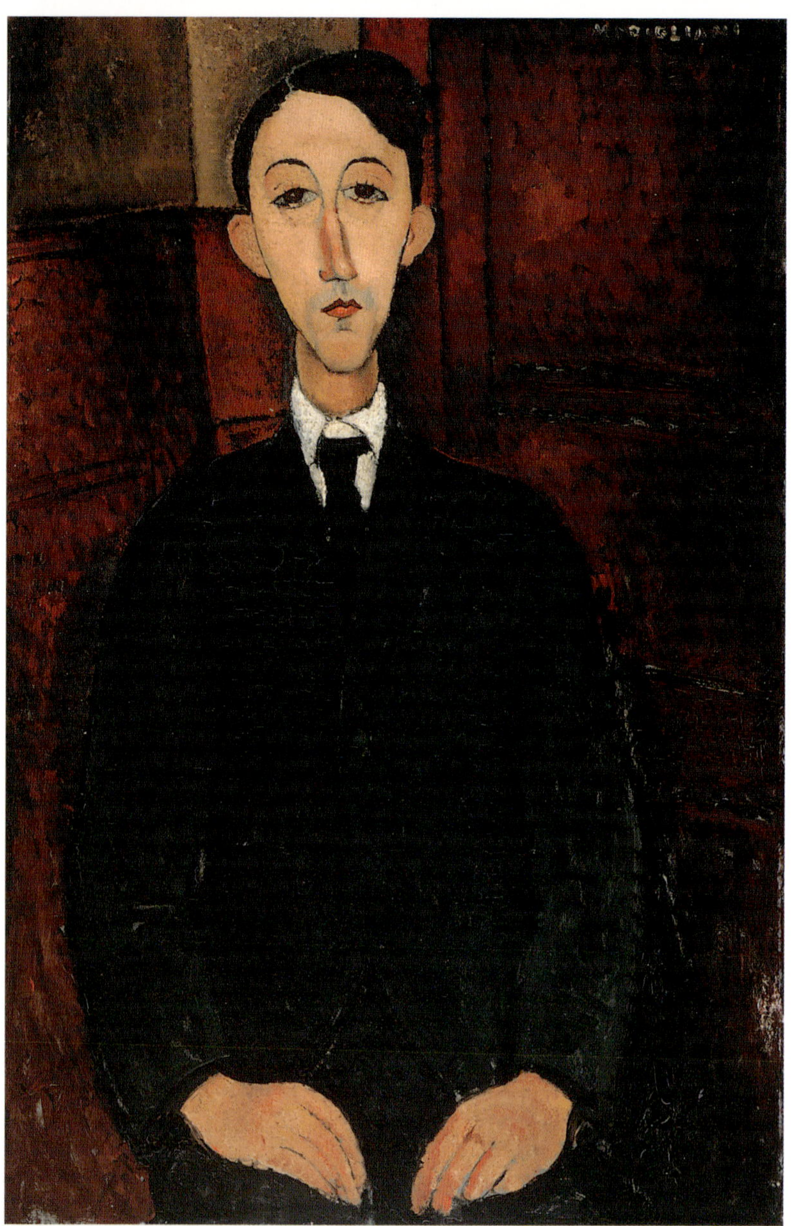

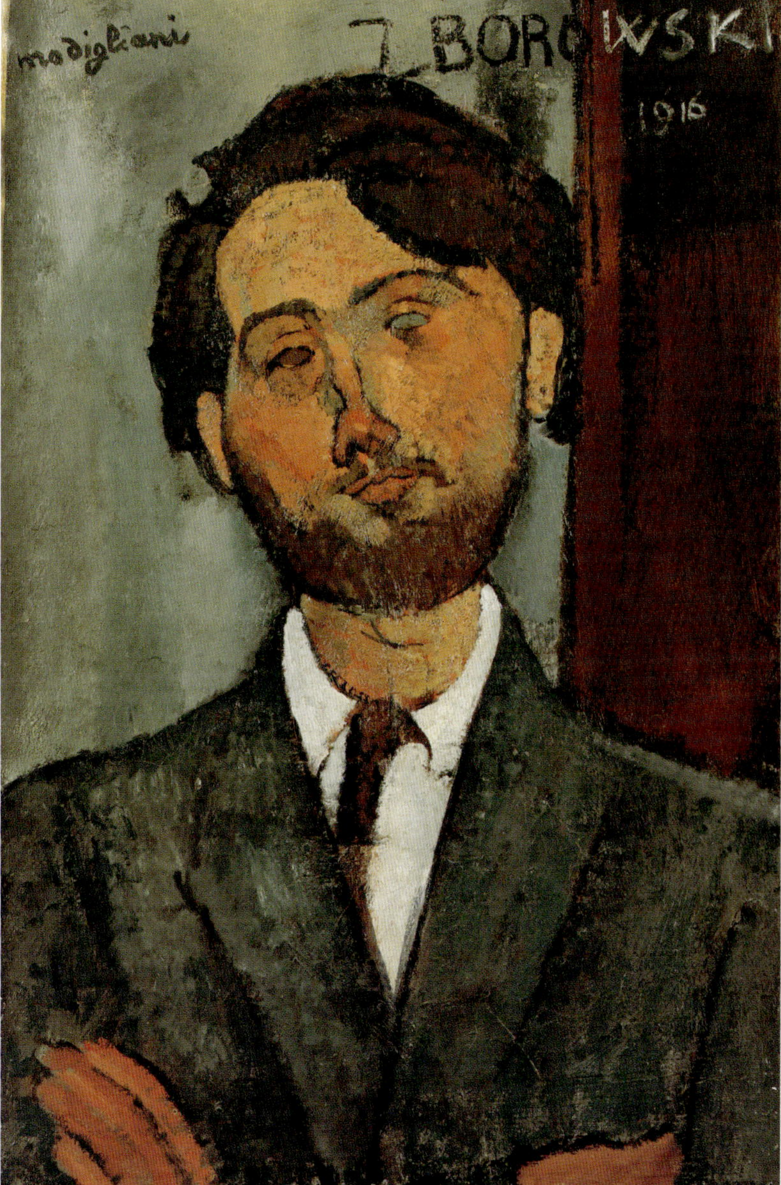

modigliani
Z. BOROWSKI
1916

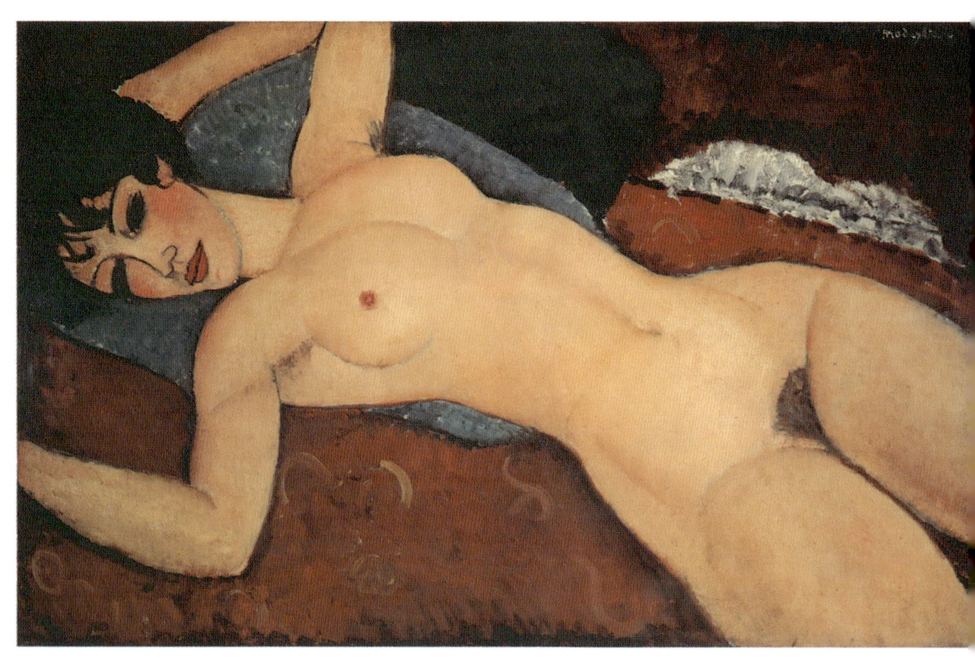

32. *Sleeping Nude with Arms
Open (Red Nude)*, 1917

33. *Comte Wielhorski*, 1917

66

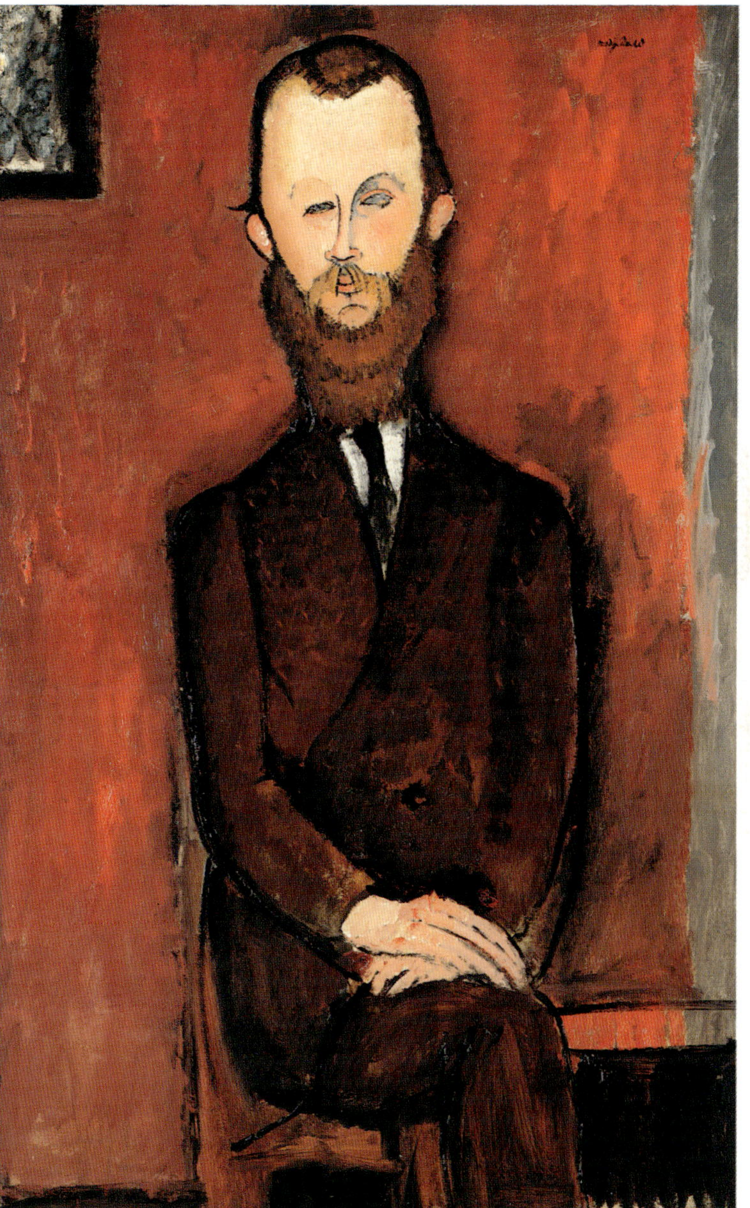

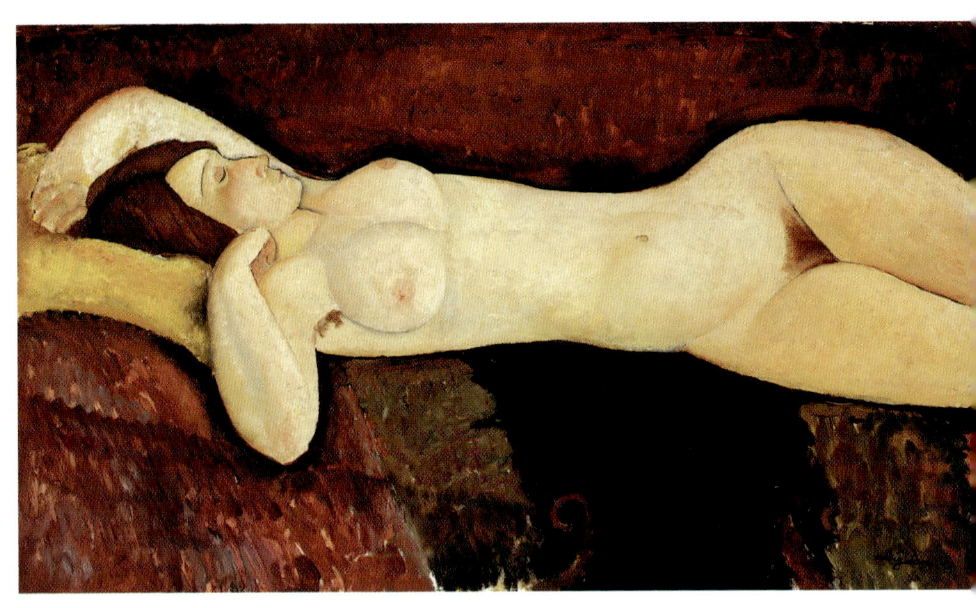

34. *Reclining Nude*
(*Grand nu couché*), *circa* 1919

35. *Hanka Zborowska*, 1917

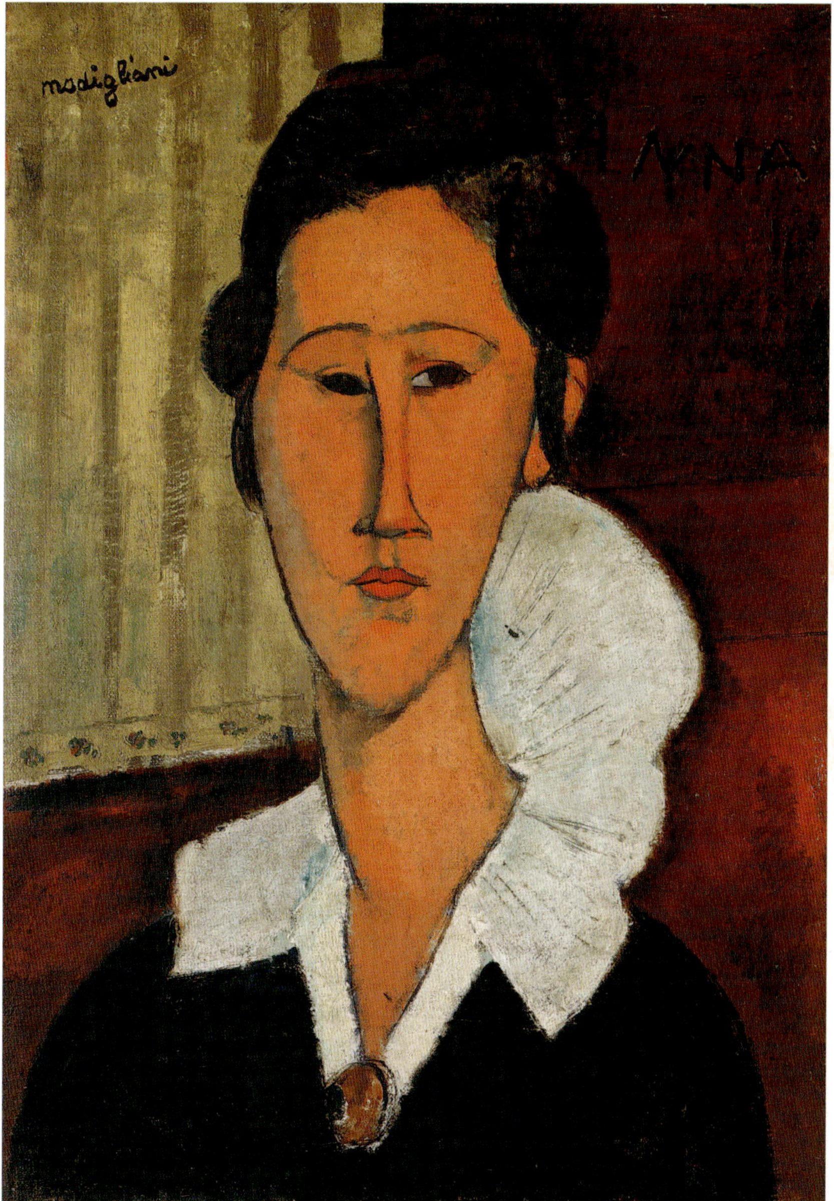

modigliani
ANNA

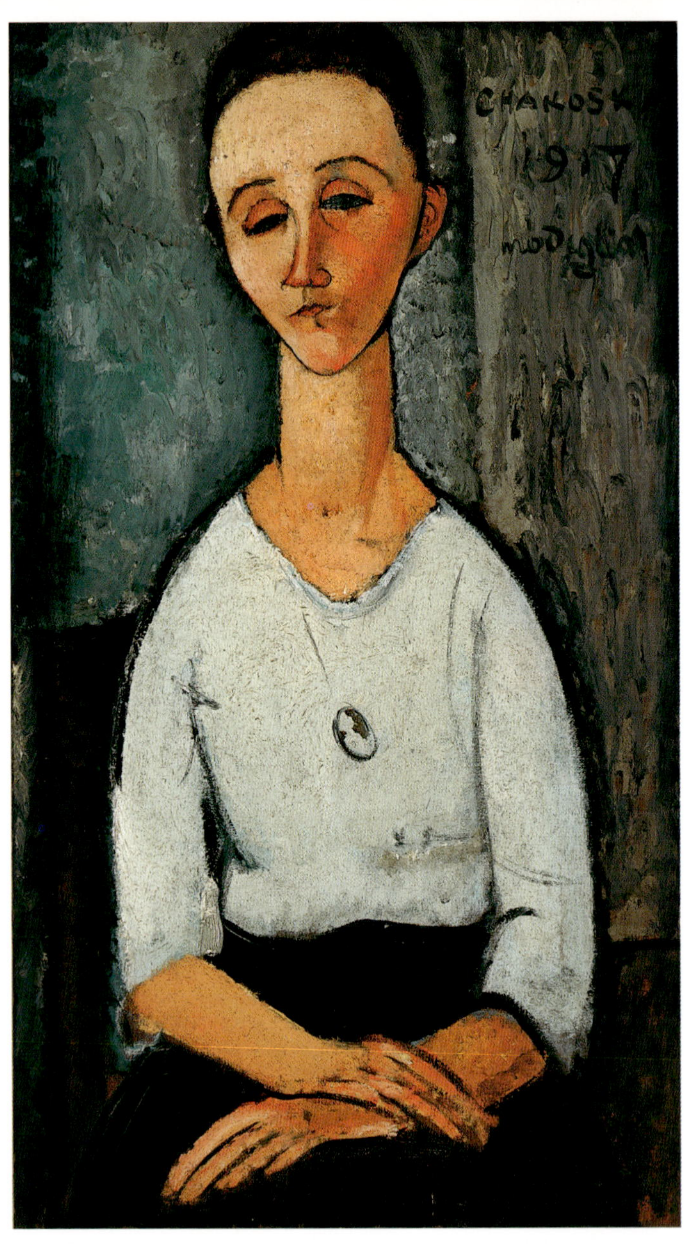

36. *Lunia Czechowska,*
1917

37. *Seated Nude with
a Shirt,* 1917

Following pages
38. *Jeanne Hébuterne
with Hat and Necklace,*
1917

39. *Lunia Czechowska,*
1917

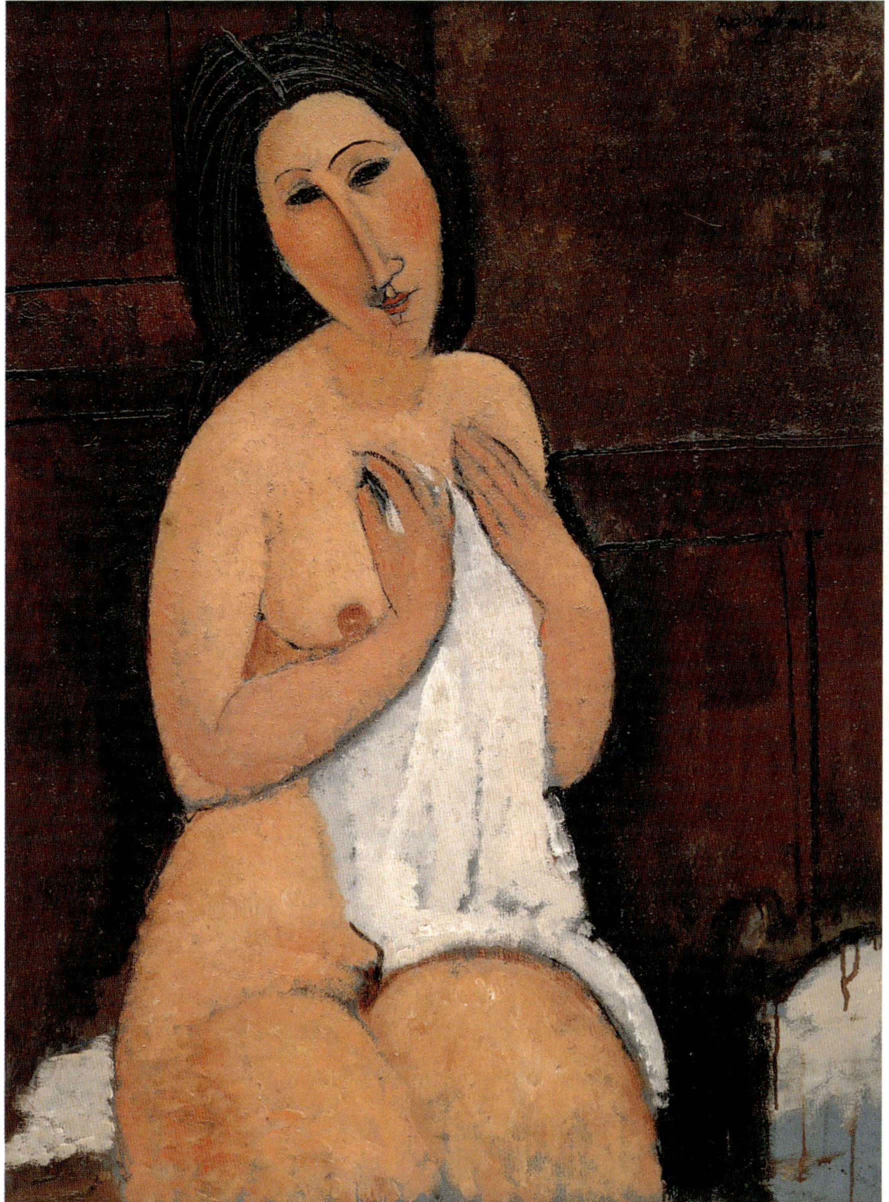

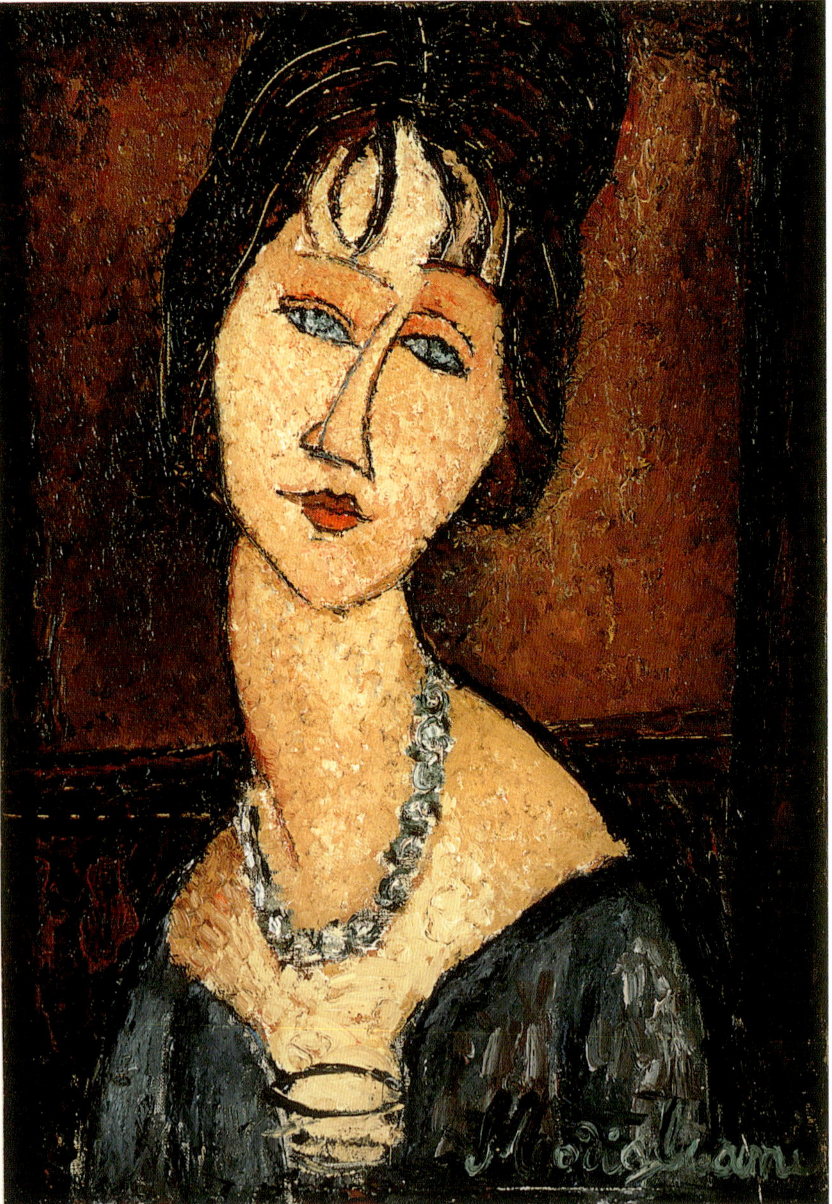

Modigliani

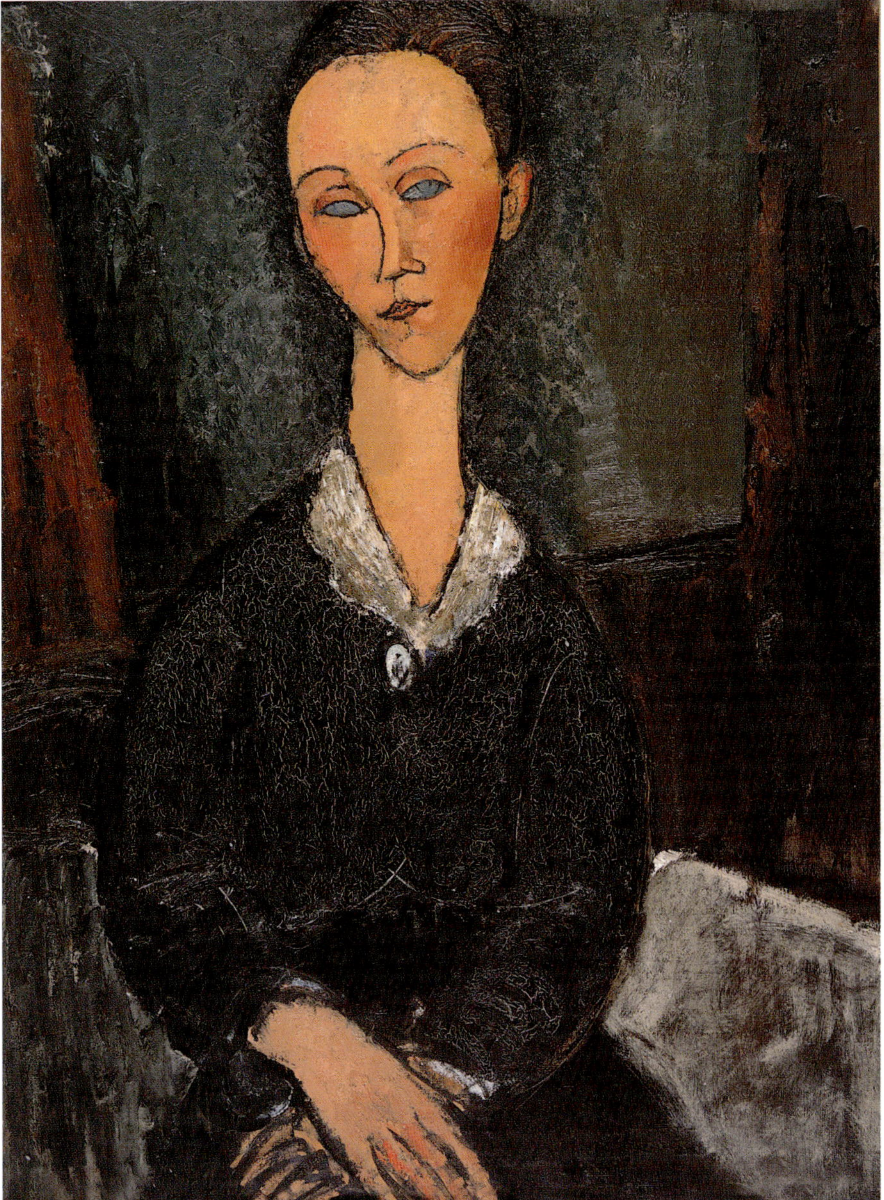

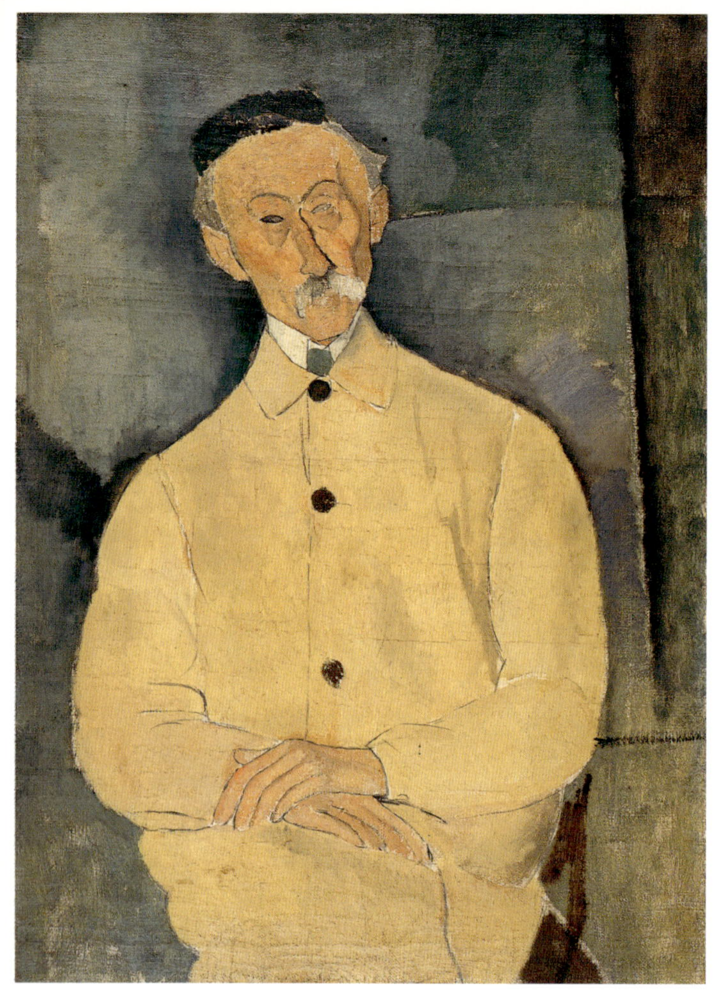

40. *Constant Lepoutre,*
1917

41. *Jeanne Hébuterne
in a Large Hat,* 1918

Following pages

42. *Jeanne Hébuterne,* 1918

43. *Little Girl in Blue,* 1918

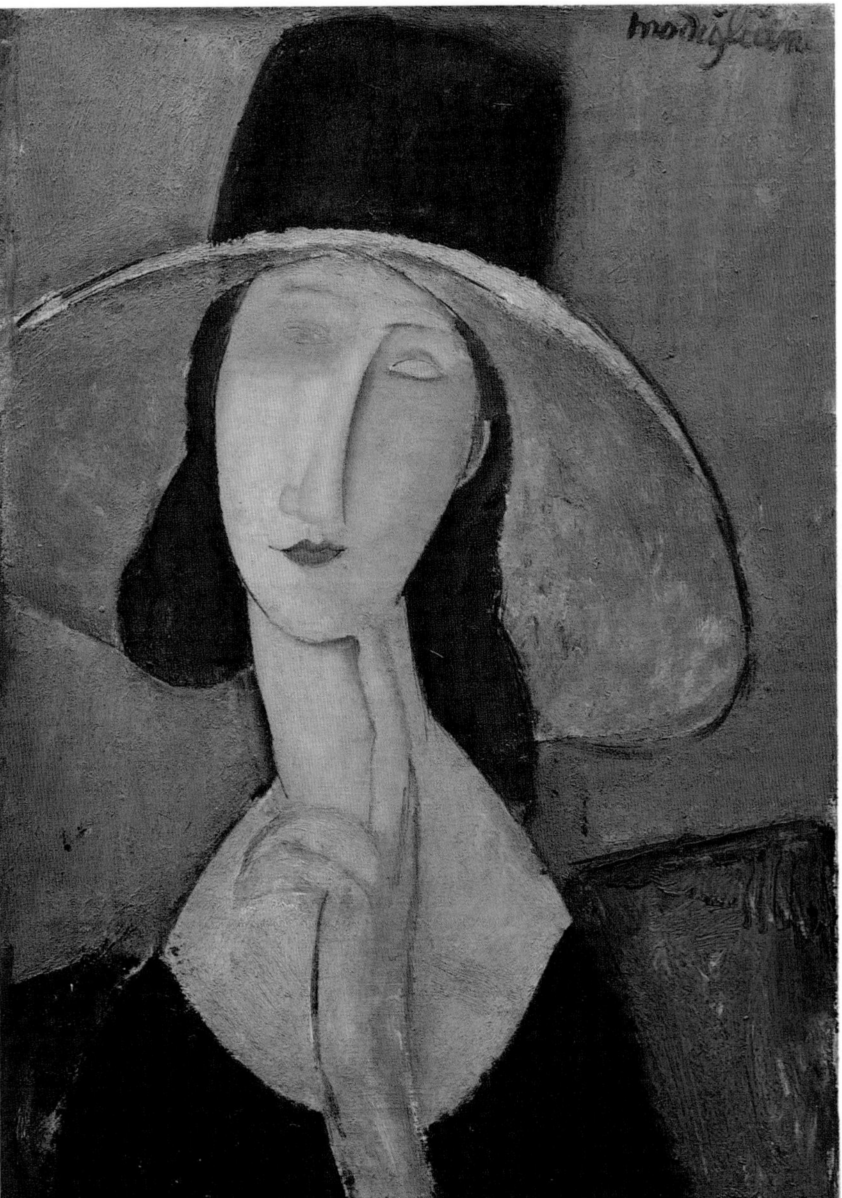

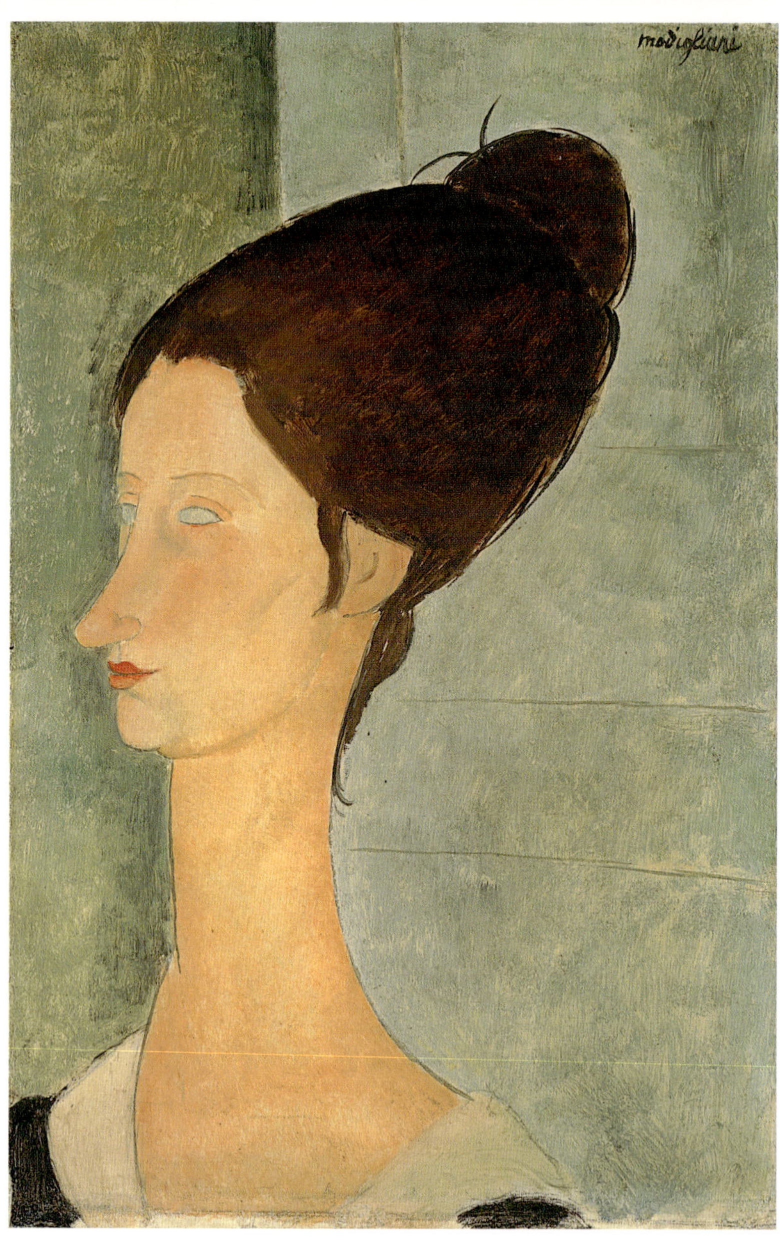

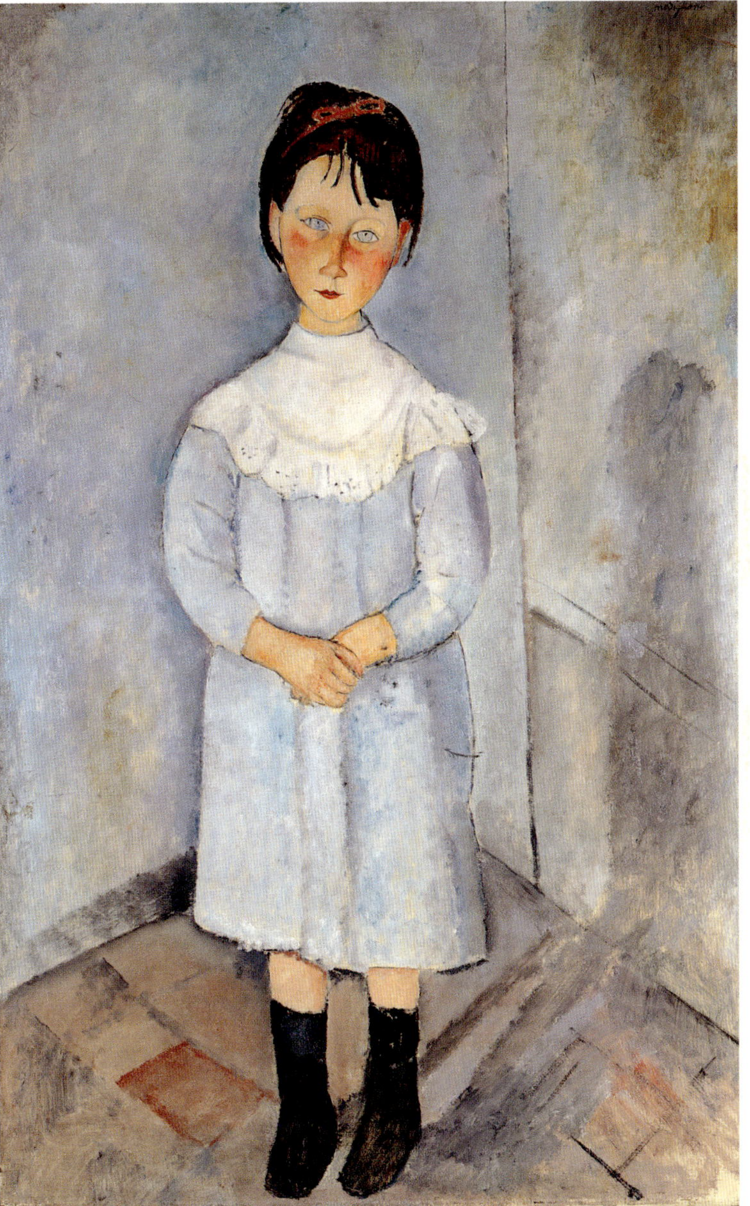

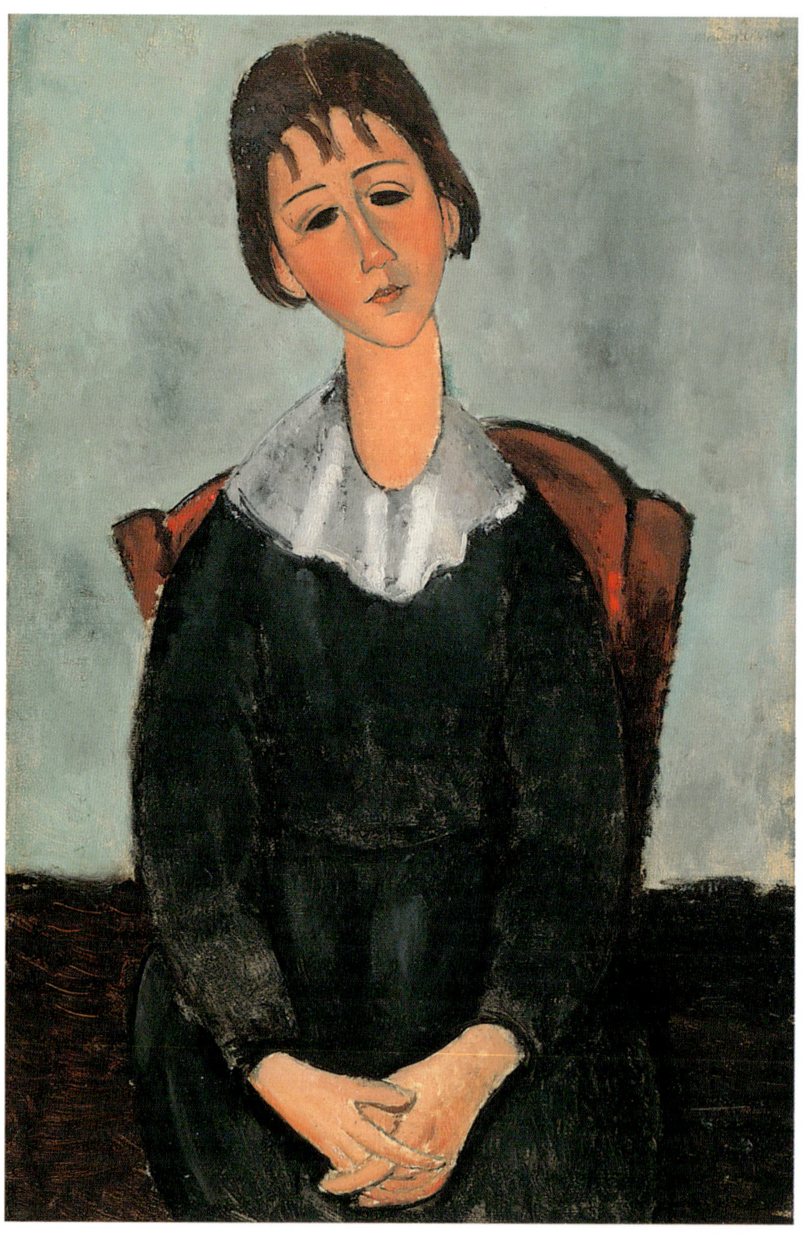

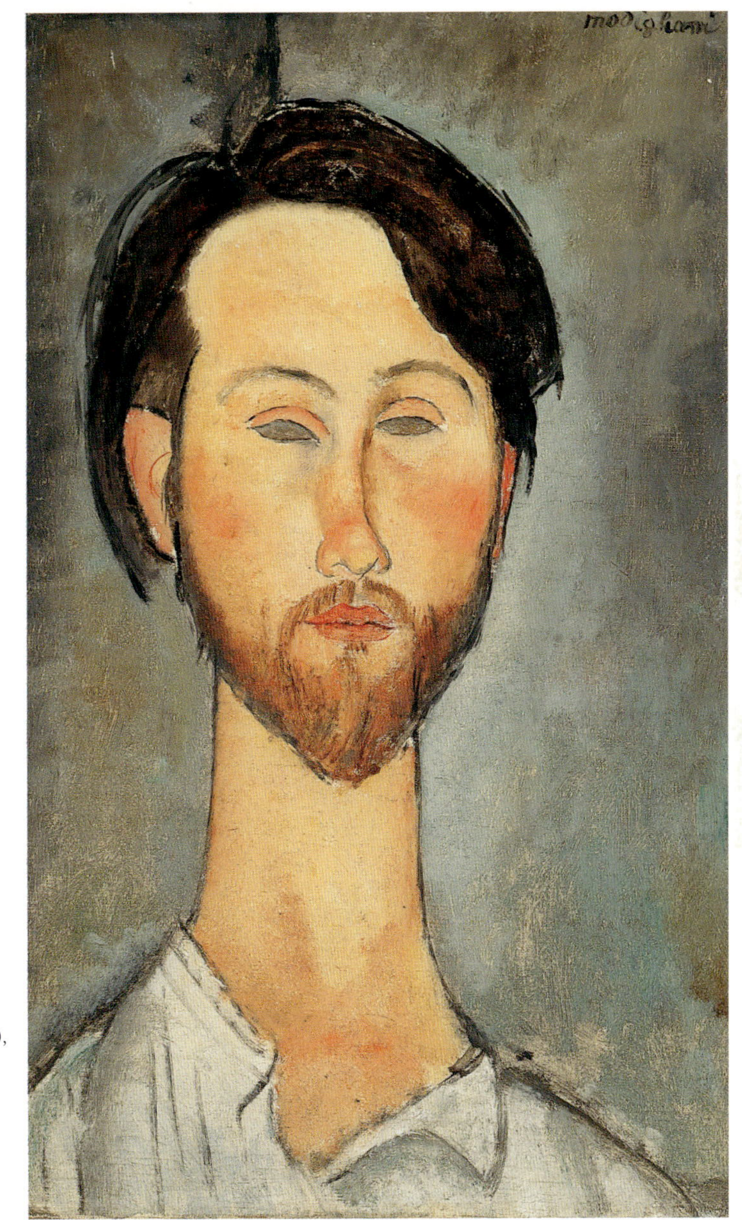

44. *Seated Girl (Mademoiselle Huguette)*, 1918

45. *Léopold Zborowski*, 1918

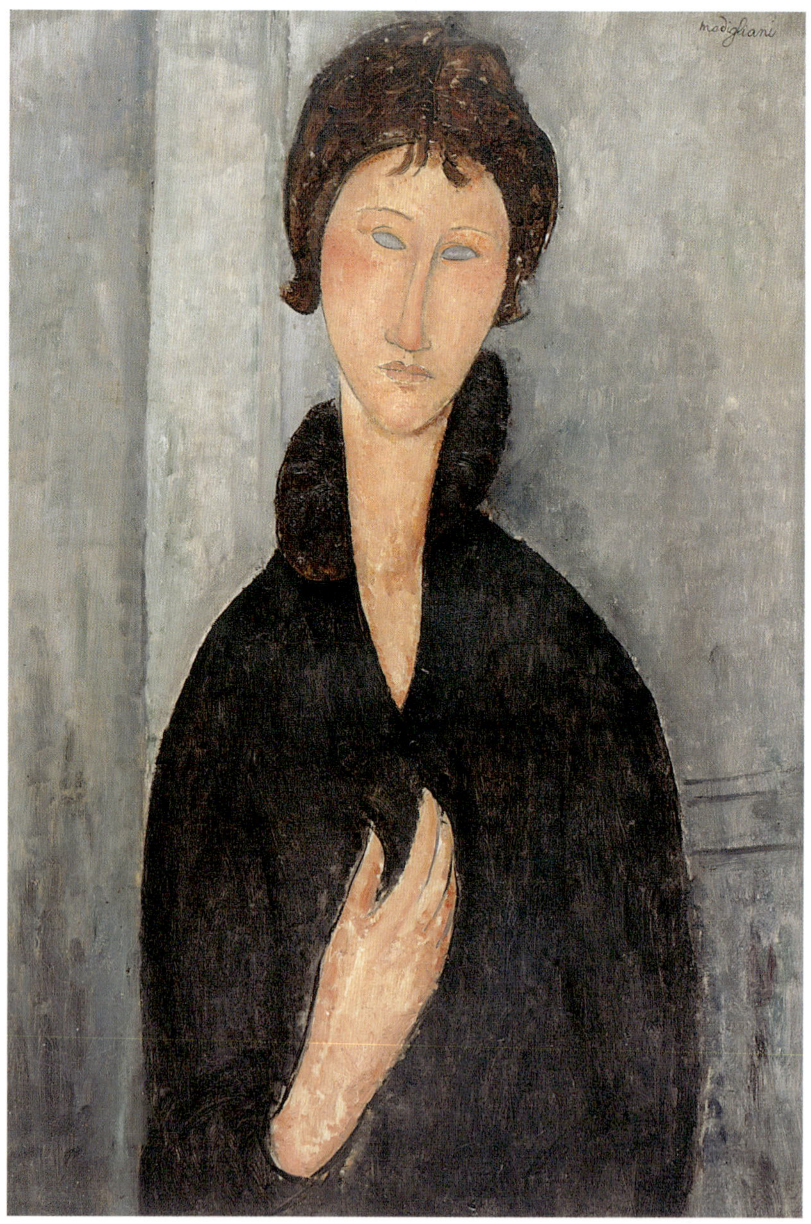
modigliani

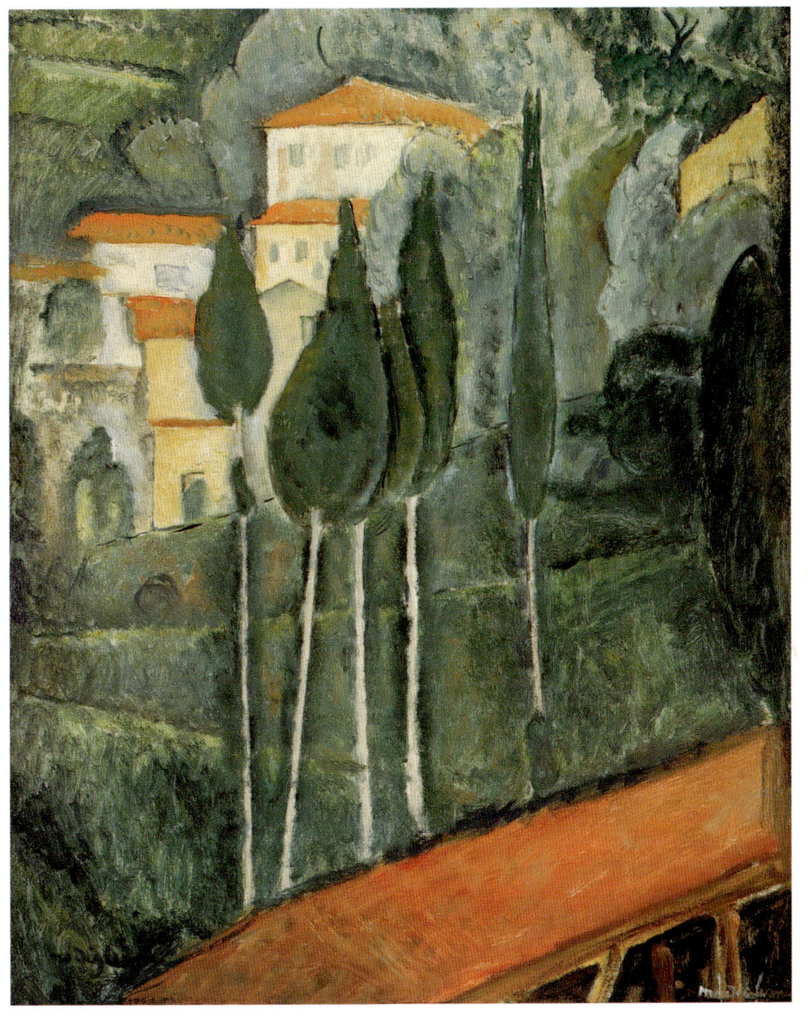

46. *Woman with Blue Eyes, 1919*

47. *Landscape, Southern France, 1919*

Following pages

48. *Roger Dutilleul, 1919*

49. *Léopold Zborowski, 1919*

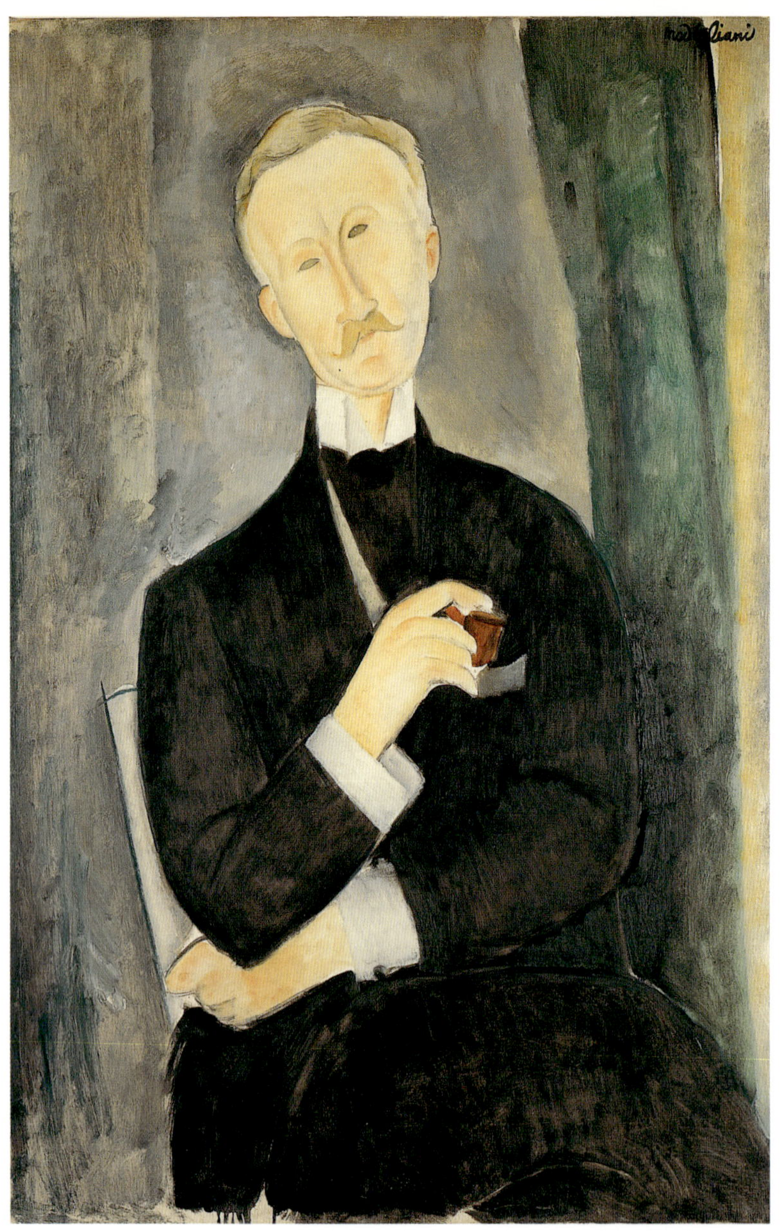

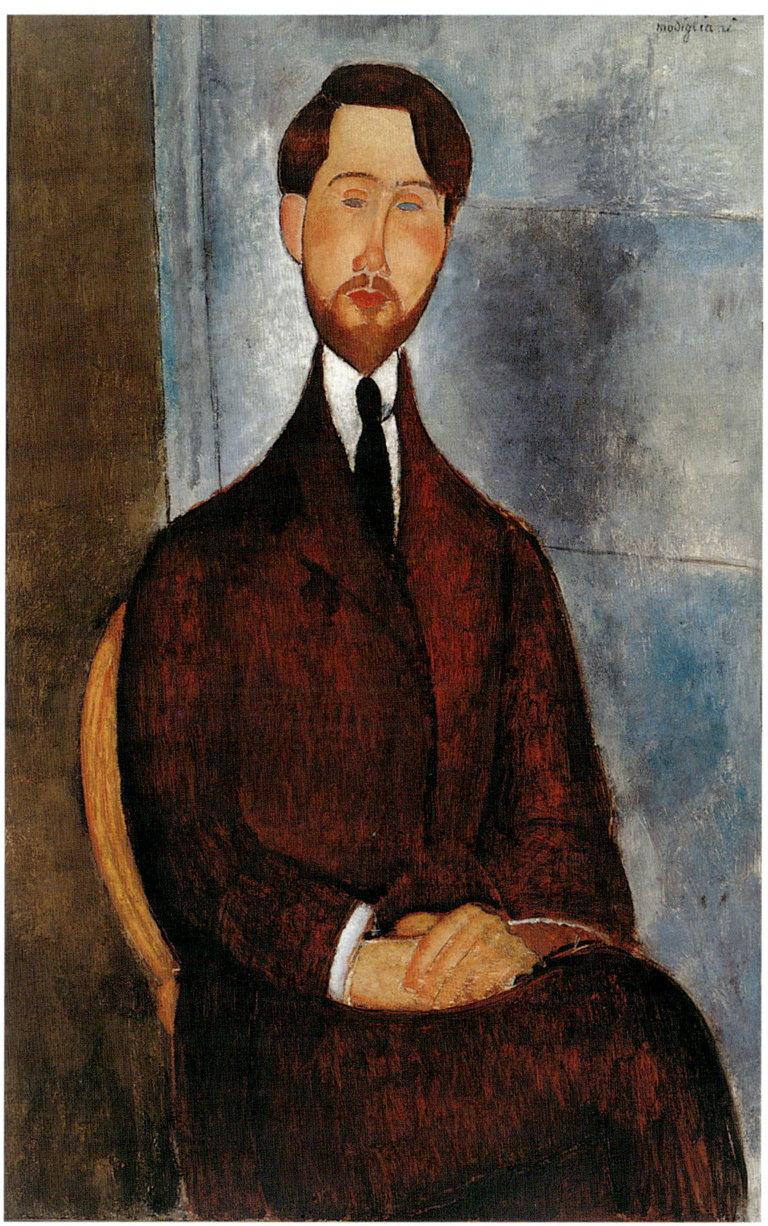

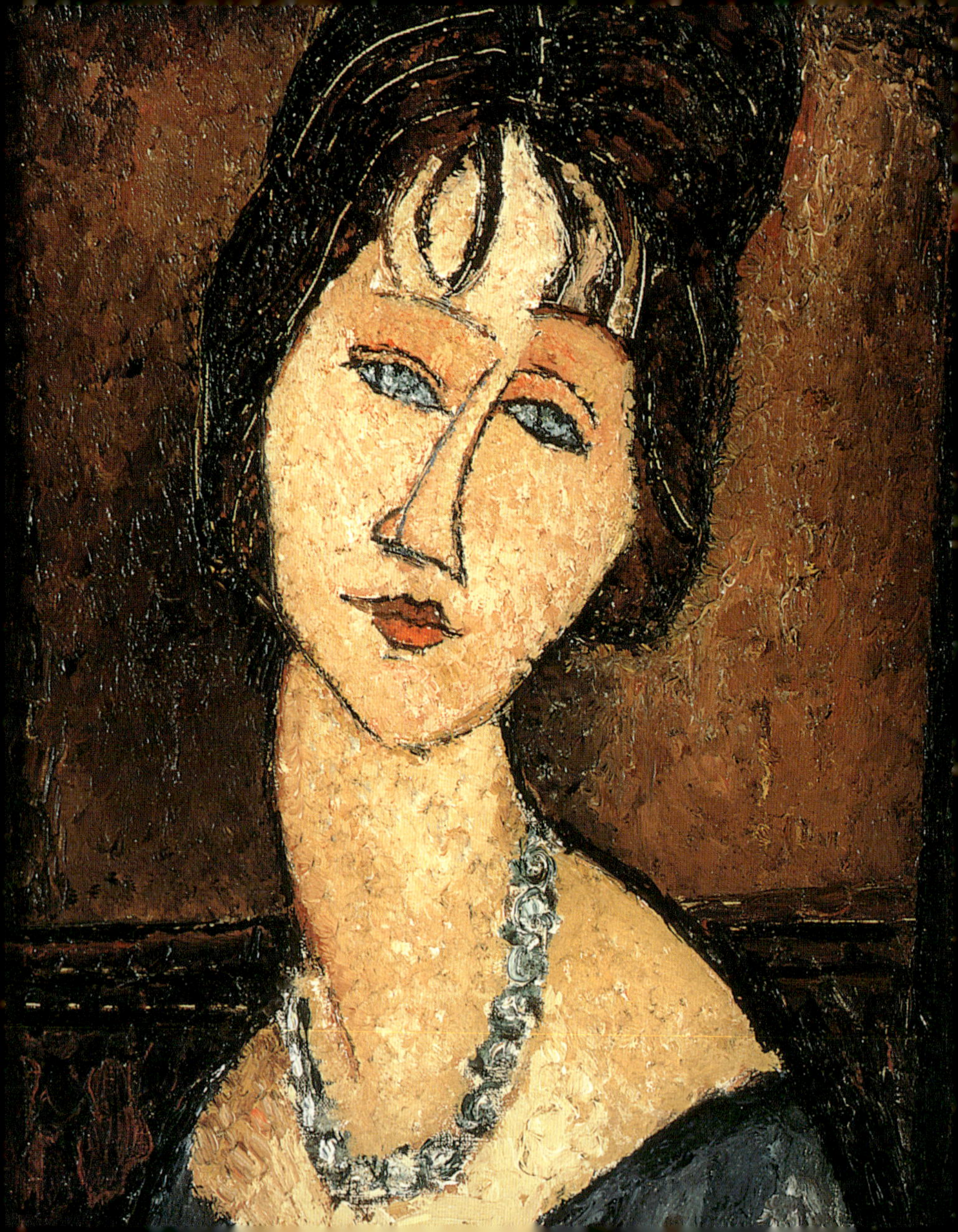

Appendix

1. *Bust of a Nude Woman*
(front), 1907-08
Oil on canvas, 80.6 x 50.1 cm
Reuben and Edith Hecht
Museum
University of Haifa, Haifa

2. *Bust of a Nude Woman*
(back): *Maud Abrantes*,
1907-08
Oil on canvas, 80.6 x 50.1 cm
Reuben and Edith Hecht
Museum
University of Haifa, Haifa

3. *Maurice Drouard*, 1909
Oil on canvas, 61 x 46 cm
Private collection

4. *Jean Alexandre*
(front), 1909
Oil on canvas, 81 x 60 cm
Fondation Pierre Gianadda,
Martigny

5. *Jean Alexandre* (back):
Seated Nude, 1909
Oil on canvas, 81 x 60 cm
Fondation Pierre Gianadda,
Martigny

6. *The Beggar of Livorno*,
1909
Oil on canvas, 66 x 52.7 cm
Private collection

7. *The Beggar*, 1909
Oil on canvas, 46 x 38 cm
Private collection

8. *The Cellist*, 1909
Oil on canvas, 130 x 80 cm
Private collection
Courtesy Christie's, London

9. *Joseph Lévi*, 1910
Oil on canvas, 53.7 x 48.7 cm
Private collection, New York

10. *Portrait of a Man with Hat*
(*José Pacheco?*), 1910-11
Oil on canvas, 65 x 54 cm
Private collection

11. *Bust of a Young Woman*,
1911
Oil on canvas, 55 x 38 cm
Frances and Bernard Laterman
Collection, New York

12. *Caryatid* (*Mademoiselle
Grain de Café*), 1911-12
Oil on canvas, 72.5 x 50 cm
Kunstsammlung Nordrhein-
Westfalen, Düsseldorf

13. *Caryatid*, 1913
Oil on canvas, 81 x 45 cm
Private collection

14. *Big Red Bust*, 1913
Oil on cardboard, 81.5 x 51 cm
Private collection

15. *Beatrice Hastings*, 1914
Oil on canvas, 58 x 37 cm
Private collection

16. *Head of a Woman*, 1915
Oil on canvas, 46 x 38 cm
Pinacoteca di Brera, Milan
Emilio and Maria Jesi Donation

17. *Head of a Woman
with Red Hair*, 1915
Oil on canvas, 46 x 38 cm
Galleria Civica d'Arte Moderna
e Contemporanea, Turin

18. *Chéron*, 1915
Oil on canvas, 46.5 x 33 cm
Private collection

19. *Pierre Reverdy*, 1915
Oil on canvas, 40.7 x 33.7 cm
Thalheimer Coleman Collection,
Baltimore on loan to the
Baltimore Museum of Art

20. *L'enfant gras*
(*The Fat Child*), 1915
Oil on canvas, 45.5 x 37.5 cm
Pinacoteca di Brera, Milan

21. *Raimondo*, 1915
Oil on paper, 51.5 x 33 cm
Art Institute, Chicago
Alsdorf Collection

22. *Madam Pompadour*
(*Portrait of Beatrice Hastings*),
1915
Oil on canvas, 60.6 x 49.5 cm
Art Institute, Chicago
Joseph Winterbotham
Collection

23. *Moïse Kisling*, 1915
Oil on canvas, 37 x 29 cm
Pinacoteca di Brera, Milan
Emilio and Maria Jesi Donation

24. *Pierrot* (*Self-Portrait in Pierrot Costume*), 1915
Oil on cardboard, 43 x 27 cm
Statens Museum for Kunst, Copenhagen
F. Rump Collection

25. *Head of a Woman with Velvet Ribbon* (*The Black Border*), 1915
Oil on paper glued onto cardboard, 54 x 45.5 cm
Musée de l'Orangerie, Paris
Walter-Guillaume Collection

26. *Léon Indenbaum*, 1915
Oil on canvas, 54.6 x 45.7 cm
Henry and Rose Pearlman Foundation, New York

27. *Antonia*, 1915
Oil on canvas, 82 x 46 cm
Musée de l'Orangerie, Paris
Walter-Guillaume Collection

28. *The Maid*, 1915
Oil on canvas, 81 x 46 cm
Private collection

29. *Paul Guillaume Seated*, 1916
Oil on canvas, 81 x 54 cm
Civico Museo d'Arte Contemporanea, Milan

30. *Manuel Humbert Estève*, 1916
Oil on canvas, 100.2 x 65.5 cm
National Gallery of Victoria, Melbourne

31. *Léopold Zborowski*, 1916
Oil on canvas, 65 x 43 cm
Private collection

32. *Sleeping Nude with Arms Open* (*Red Nude*), 1917
Oil on canvas, 60 x 92 cm
Mattioli Collection, Milan

33. *Comte Wielhorski*, 1917
Oil on canvas, 114 x 72 cm
Private collection

34. *Reclining Nude* (*Grand nu couché*), *circa* 1919
Oil on canvas, 73 x 116 cm
The Museum of Modern Art, New York

35. *Hanka Zborowska*, 1917
Oil on canvas, 55 x 38 cm
Galleria Nazionale d'Arte Moderna e Contemporanea, Rome

36. *Lunia Czechowska*, 1917
Oil on canvas, 81 x 45 cm
Museu de Arte de São Paulo, São Paulo
Assis Chateaubriand

37. *Seated Nude with a Shirt*, 1917
Oil on canvas, 92 x 67.5 cm
Musée d'Art moderne, Villeneuve-d'Ascq
Geneviève and Jean Masurel Donation

38. *Jeanne Hébuterne with Hat and Necklace*, 1917
Oil on canvas, 55.5 x 38.5 cm
Private collection

39. *Lunia Czechowska*, 1917
Oil on canvas, 81 x 60.2 cm
Musée de Grenoble, Grenoble

40. *Constant Lepoutre*, 1917
Oil on canvas, 92 x 65 cm
Private collection

41. *Jeanne Hébuterne in a Large Hat*, 1918
Oil on canvas, 55 x 38 cm
Private collection, Japan

42. *Jeanne Hébuterne*, 1918
Oil on canvas, 47 x 33 cm
Private collection

43. *Little Girl in Blue*, 1918
Oil on canvas, 116 x 73 cm
Private collection

44. *Seated Girl* (*Mademoiselle Huguette*), 1918
Oil on canvas, 91.4 x 60.3 cm
Asahi Breweries, Ltd., Tokyo

45. *Léopold Zborowski*, 1918
Oil on canvas, 46 x 27 cm
Private collection

46. *Woman with Blue Eyes*, 1919
Oil on canvas, 81 x 54 cm
Musée d'Art moderne de la Ville de Paris, Paris

47. *Landscape, Southern France*, 1919
Oil on canvas, 60 x 45 cm
M. Schecter Collection

48. *Roger Dutilleul*, 1919
Oil on canvas, 100 x 65 cm
Private collection

49. *Léopold Zborowski*, 1919
Oil on canvas, 100 x 64 cm
Museu de Arte de São Paulo, São Paulo
Assis Chateaubriand

	Life of Modigliani	Historical Events
1884	Amedeo Modigliani is born in Livorno on 12 July.	Huysmans brings out *À rebours*. Guyau's *Problèmes of esthétique contemporaine* is published.
1895	He recovers from a serious attack of pleurisy that will have repercussions on his health for the rest of his life.	The Lumière brothers develop the first film camera and projector. Röntgen takes the first X-ray photograph.
1897	He begins a course of drawing lessons in August.	
1898	He suffers from pulmonary complications. He gives up his studies and frequents the studio of Guglielmo Micheli, who had been a pupil of Giovanni Fattori.	
1901	He visits Rome and Florence.	Queen Victoria dies in England. Giuseppe Verdi dies in Milan. Picasso's so-called "Blue Period" begins.
1902	He enrols in the Scuola Libera di Nudo in Florence.	Zola dies.
1903	He enrols in the Scuola Libera di Nudo at the Istituto delle Belle Arti in Venice.	
1904		Picasso moves to Paris for good.
1906	In the winter he moves to Paris. He rents a studio in Rue Caulaincourt, at Montmartre, not far from Le Bateau-Lavoir.	The "Dreyfus Affair" erupts. Cézanne dies on 22 October.
1907	He meets Doctor Paul Alexandre, who becomes his admirer and collector.	Bergson publishes *Creative Evolution*. Picasso paints *Les Demoiselles d'Avignon*.
1908	He shows six works at the Salon des Indépendants, including *The Jewess* and *Bust of a Nude Woman*.	In Paris, memorable soirée at the Bateau-Lavoir in honour of Henri Rousseau.

	Life of Modigliani	**Historical Events**
1909	He paints portraits of Paul Alexandre, his father and his brother. In the summer he goes back to Livorno. Returning to Paris he brings with him *The Beggar*. Paul Alexandre introduces him to Brancusi.	Marconi wins the Nobel Prize for the development of the wireless telegraph. The first Futurist manifesto is published in Paris.
1910	He draws and starts to work stone regularly. He meets Anna Akhmatova, with whom he begins an intense relationship.	Pius X requires clerics to take an oath denouncing Modernism. Braque paints *Violin and Palette*, creating the illusion of a nail that casts a shadow; Kandinsky works on the text *Concerning the Spiritual in Art*.
1912	He exhibits eight stone sculptures at the 10th Salon d'Automne.	Sinking of the *Titanic* on her maiden voyage. Duchamp works on *Nude Descending a Staircase*.
1914	Paul Alexandre is called up for the army. Modigliani meets Beatrice Hastings.	Archduke Franz Ferdinand of Austria is assassinated in Sarajevo: the Great War commences.
1915	Max Jacob introduces him to Paul Guillaume, art connoisseur and dealer.	Italy goes to war with Austria. Dada is born in Zurich.
1917	He meets Jeanne Hébuterne. His first solo exhibition is held at Berthe Weill's gallery. The police call for withdrawal of the nudes.	Italian defeat at Caporetto. The United States enters the war. Revolution in Russia.
1918	He goes to the Côte d'Azur. Jeanne is pregnant. A baby girl is born on 29 November, and only later is registered under the name Jeanne Modigliani.	Italian victory at Vittorio Veneto.
1919	He returns to Paris.	Peace conference in Paris: the League of Nations is set up.
1920	He dies at the Hôpital de la Charité. In a letter to his family, Zborowski writes: "His companion (…) has not survived him: the day after his death (…) she threw herself from the fifth-floor window of her parent's house, dying instantly".	The Fascists use organized violence against their political adversaries in Italy. The Kapp Putsch in Germany. Foundation of the Communist Party in France.

Critical Anthology

M. Restellini

*Modigliani: Avant-Garde Artist or
"Schizophrenic painter"?*, in *Modigliani.
The Melancholy Angel*, Milan 2002
The impression [Modigliani] gave – that
of being quite out of the ordinary – was
enhanced by his close brush with death,
and explain the fascination he held for
his friends and his eventual lover, Jeanne
Hébuterne. The witnesses coincide on
this. Paul Alexandre, Modigliani's first
patron but a friend too, wrote: "The man
was as attractive as his work. (…) He
was a born aristocrat: He had the style
and all the tastes". But his friends were
also acquainted with his strong
personality and very precise ideas about
art. (…) Paul Alexandre wrote: "Modigliani
had an exclusive passion for his his art.
There was no question of turning aside
even for a moment from his life's work to
undertake what were in his eyes menial
tasks. (…) He already had a deep rooted
confidence in his own worth, he knew
that he was an innovator rather than a
follower." (…) Modigliani thus exhibited
an uncompromising elitism; he was
willing to starve rather than accept Jean
Alexandre's suggestion that he made
drawings for *L'Assiette au beurre*, a
satirical review offering excellent rates of
pay. No concession, no sacrifice of his art
could be considered. This may explain the
terrible rages to which he was subject,
and which contributed to his reputation
for violence. According to the legend,
drink and drugs fuelled these outbursts,
whereas the principal trigger was the
incomprehension of those around him.
(…) Modigliani's uncompromisingly elitist
vision of the creative life was nothing
new for him; as early as 1901 he had
expressed himself in similar terms to his
friend Ghiglia. And this vision was not
political, but a private philosophy, based
partly on the sense of the superiority of
the artist and partly on his sense of the
value of his art. Modigliani felt that he
was different from other and perhaps
superior to them. He frequently quoted
a tag from D'Annunzio, which he wrote
on the back of certain graphic works:
"Life is a Gift: from the few to the many:
from Those who Know and Have to those
who neither Know nor Have".
One explanation of this sense of
superiority may of course have been
Modigliani's confrontation with illness and
death: he had not only survived typhoid
fever, but apparently vanquished
tuberculosis too. He had seen the
imminence of his own death, and live
to tell the tale. This necessarily gave him
a unique vision of life and other human
beings, a vision exacerbated by his
extreme sensitivity and early exposure
to poetry. That vision haunted him for the
rest of his life. The last message that he
wrote to Paul Alexandre (May 6, 1913)
runs: Toady and friend / Happiness is
a grave-faced angel / The resuscitated
[man].

B. Dorival

Painters' Sculpture, in *Modigliani.
The Melancholy Angel*, Milan 2002
The interest that painters take in
sculpture in one of the most curious
aspects of contemporary art. Painters
who sculpted were extremely rare in the
seventeenth and eighteenth centuries.
And the nineteenth century itself, though
rich in sculptor-painters – the greatest

names are those of Barye and Carpeaux – could count few painter-sculptors; Géricault, Daumier and Degas are honourable exceptions to this rule. But in the wake of Gauguin, who – in this as in so many other matters – led the way, almost all the great masters of pictorial art now also wield the chisel. Gauguin's experimentality ad formal accomplishment are echoed in Modigliani (…). Sculpting is, however, and expensive businness, and sculptures are even more difficult to "place" than paintings and drawings. So, to earn a living, Modigliani was compelled to paint and draw, driven by a cruel fate to abandon the art for which he was born. Throughout his life, sculpture remained his dream. A large part of his painted work and still more of his graphic corpus consists of projected statues that he could never afford to realize. I am thinking in particular of the many sketches of *Caryatids* that constitute some of the finest of his youthful works. He did, at the same time, carved stone figures, though many fewer than he might have wished.

(…) [Modigliani's] work demonstrates the precious new blood infused into sculpture by the painters' formal experiments. From the sixteenth century on, Western sculpture had focused exclusively on classical Greece. The modern painters, in their sculptures, opened that art to other sources of inspiration: sources as diverse as French Medieval, Chinese, Cambodian, Indian and Central Asian statuary. They were a fountain of youth for the art. Broadening its horizons, the painters taught sculpture, as they had thaught painting, to confront fundamental challenges, notably that of its own nature. Their own example vindicated experiments such as that of pure sculpture. The turn taken by modern sculpture – audacity, experiment and renewal – came about because this was the direction the painters suggested.

F. Carco

"Modigliani", in *L'Eventail*, 15 July 1919
Some nudes, various portraits… We are never going to see, I think, Modigliani tackle other themes.

But the portraits, like the nudes, that he has painted straight off, against backdrops chosen at random, are sufficient to ennoble his art. If this strikes you by its cynicism and by the employment of a palette that he reduces to two or three tones treated in a haphazard way; if he deforms, consumed by the desire of achieve beauty; if he makes sacrifices to create and if nothing interests him but the choice of colour, after the rhythm or this secret architecture of the movement 'that subordinates the lines', are you not equally struck by your slowness in grasping the subtle relations between the painter's sensibility and the very object of his attraction? It is not his realism, in the sense that it is normally understood in painting, that is in doubt, even though it does not seem to me that such intensity has ever been attained in a woman's face prior to Modigliani (…). I have watched Modigliani drawing. His acute sense of shading leads him to model the join of an arm, the pure curve of a youthful breast; he concentrates complex structures into a single, barely perceptible one, sustains the slight bulge of a belly, extends a movement right to the heart of the soul, lets it come to life (…). I would like to express my admiration for Modigliani's drawings; every grace is realized there in style, and it is the same style that we now find in the paintings when the artist captures on the canvas his own feeling for things, his peculiar vision of the world, of rhythms and colours (…). Painter, do not forget the necessity of the arts to respect the conventions on which they are based and that unite them. Thus the plastic sense of forms, determined by him through values that are balanced by dint of planes rather than colour, is evident in Modigliani right from the first encounter with his work, and with such a force that it has been possible for him to change his modes of expression without in any way disturbing the character of his painting.

If he once used to bring out the tormented relief of a face from bituminous backgrounds dense in volumes; if this face, for its part, was no more than an object of secondary importance of which he coordinated the essential traits, then it is necessary to acknowledge the extent to which Modigliani's ideas have evolved in this sense. The backgrounds have grown lighter; they have grown animated; they are nourished by a multitude of gradations, while their nobility without affectation participates in the life of the composition. The figure itself reveals a new spirit. The light, finally, that our painter wanted more or less even everywhere, makes the line explode, rendering it more sensitive and, despite his respect for the arabesque, opening it up to rarer subtleties. It has been said of Modigliani that his deformations no longer clashed with the sense that one had of the human figure; this in no way means that he has renounced the trends in his own art. He has simply dug deeper into the resources that a painter can obtain from the palette and has made use of them. Whence the evident revolution that has taken place in his painting; I would even say, the elevation of it.

L. Vitali
Disegni di Modigliani, 1929
The fact is that the key to Modigliani's art,

the *raison d'être* of the deformations to which he subjects his models (with their elongated faces, tilted on cylindrical necks that support the heads almost in the manner of a column), the sense of spiritual lightness that emanates from his works, a delight that I can only compare to that of the harmonious figures of a slow dance, have only one name: arabesque. For this reason it seems to me that Modigliani – in a certain sense, for the artist remains of our own time (the one that comes in a direct line from Baudelaire and Rimbaud) and in this lies his virtue – belongs to the same family out of which came the Japanese and two Italians who have expressed themselves in the same pictorial language: I am speaking of Simone Martini and Sandro Botticelli. But it is above all with the Sienese artist that I like to compare Modigliani: with Simone Martini, when he abandons narration to become a decorative painter (decorative, in Berenson's sense). (…)

The drawing of a painter is like the private diary of a writer; in it the artist reveals himself to you frankly, in his essential characteristics, without simulation and without tricks, which in any case the aristocratic contrast of black and white would hardly allow. (…)

It is rare to find a preoccupation with chiaroscuro in them; very often it is a thin and even line, that runs lightly without a break, with singular purity, enclosing the forms in a well cadenced play of arabesques of an exquisite elegance. The curves intertwine and gradually combine with an almost musical feeling, between pauses and resumptions, intersections and suspensions; suggesting more than describing, summarizing and not analyzing. And in the same way as the melody of a shepherd's flute evokes with its modulated cadences a whole ideal world of nostalgia, Modigliani's arabesque surpasses the minute reality of the model, lifting it into a different and higher world, where women endowed with a strange languor have bodies of virginal purity.

L. Venturi

from the catalogue of the Venice Biennale, 1930
Everything is reflected in his art, grandeur and generosity as well as sensual violence. But since it is art, its virtue and its vices can no longer be reduced to positive and negative, as in moral life. Ideal aspirations have contributed as much to the creation of his artistic fantasy as have sensual deviations. Indeed their substance has produced what is seen today as the wonderful equilibrium of his art. I have heard the most conflicting opinions about Modigliani's nudes: some are moved by their chastity and others seem horrified by their shamelessness. And yet they are never susceptible to a moral judgement, for neither are they pieces of nature, nor are they associated with particular natures. Indeed they arrive at the fantastic reality of their forms and their colours by a parallel route. And if that fantasy is pervaded with significance, it means that Modigliani's art is not fanciful, but vibrant with concrete life (…).

R. Carrieri

Amedeo Modigliani, 1950
There have been many before him: with greater talent, with more ability, with more resistance, with more hope. There have been many who went further, before and after him.
But Modigliani is one. Modigliani is indivisible. His story begins and ends with him. And so does his painting. Modigliani is the unity of the soul. He was a terrible sinner, one of those who burn and consume everything to get to the centre of the soul. Colour was the emanation of this centre: its root and its ecstasy. When an attempt was made to theorize about his range of colours what came out was a laboratory report. To attain the anxiety of his reds Modigliani burned the candle at both ends. He sinned. He atoned. He sinned again. He sought after his red like Saint Catherine. It was a presentiment and a calling. Women were fire. Painting was fire. Paris as Babylon, the capital of evil. He saw it as red like the Sienese saw the city of the devil. And red were the faces of the women from whose eyes the departed soul breathed in the air, turning it red. When Modigliani used up the last red he died. (…)
He has neither the variability of style nor the intemperance of the School of Paris. He doesn't make a fuss about systems. He doesn't have a system. He has no ideas to impose nor to make use of. He is not a panorama like Picasso. He is like Rouault, whose love of warm tones he shares. But his burnt tone does not come from luministic adventures. His is not an erudite hand like Derain's. (…)
Monodic expression is fundamental in Modigliani's style. In the depths of his being there is something Oriental, and not just because of his Semitic origins. The tendency to the symbol and the motif, repetition, the enclosed form and colour. That marking of rhythm and cadence. The elegance of the unbroken line that verges on stylization. That way of emphasizing the line and making it pliable in the most melodious curves. The very insistence of some effusions.
The precision of his returns and the limited range of his repertoire, reduced to a single and easily recognizable typology. His fidelity to the human figure elevated to image.

Selected Bibliography

A. Basler, *Modigliani*, Paris 1931

B. Nicholson, *Modigliani, Paintings*, London 1948

J. Cocteau, *Modigliani*, Paris 1950

M. Raynal, *Modigliani*, Geneve-Paris-New York 1951

A. Ceroni, *Amedeo Modigliani peintre, suivi des "Souvenirs" de Lunia Czechowska*, Milan 1958

J. Modigliani, *Modigliani, Man and Myth*, New York 1958

P. Sichel, *A Biography of Amedeo Modigliani*, New York 1967

N. Ponente, *Modigliani: the life and work of the artist*, London 1969

H.I. Hubbard, *Modigliani and the painters of Montparnasse*, Milan-New York 1970

A. Ceroni, *Tout l'œuvre peint de Modigliani*, Paris 1972

C. Mann, *Modigliani*, London 1980

A. Werner, *Amedeo Modigliani*, London 1990

W. Schmalenbach (edited by), *Amedeo Modigliani*, Düsseldorf 1991

N. Alexandre, *The Unknown Modigliani: Drawings from the collection of Paul Alexandre*, exhibition catalogue, New York 1993

A. Kruszynski, *Amedeo Modigliani, Portraits and Nudes*, London 1996

D. Krystof, *Amedeo Modigliani, 1884-1920. The Poetry of Seeing*, London 1996

R. Chiappini (edited by), *Amedeo Modigliani*, Milan 1999

M. Restellini (edited by), *Amedeo Modigliani. The Melancholy Angel*, exhibition catalogue, Milan 2002

R. Chiappini (edited by), *Modigliani*, exhibition catalogue, Milan 2006

S. Fraquelli, N. Rosenthal (edited by), *Modigliani and his models*, exhibition catalogue, London 2006

J. Meyers, *Modigliani: a life*, San Diego-London 2006

N. Wolf, *Amedeo Modigliani: Erotic Sketches*, London 2008